**OFI**

# NATIONAL BASKETBALL ASSOCIATION

## 2003-2004

### BASKETBALL OPERATIONS DEPT.

Stu Jackson, Senior Vice President, Basketball Operations

Published by THE SPORTING NEWS, a division of Vulcan Sports Media,
St. Louis, Missouri 63132

Copyright © 2003 NBA Properties, Inc.

All rights reserved.

# RULES INDEX

| | RULE | SECTION | ARTICLE | PAGE |
|---|---|---|---|---|
| **BACKCOURT/FRONTCOURT** | | | | |
| Definitions | 4 | VI | a & b | 18 |
| Eight (8) Second Violation | 4 | VI | f | 18 |
| Player Position Status | 4 | VI | c | 18 |
| Ball Position Status | 4 | VI | d & e | 18 |
| **BALL** | | | | |
| Dead Ball | 6 | IV | a | 26 |
| Jump—Center Circle | 6 | V | | 26 |
| Jump—Free Throw Circle | 6 | VI | | 27 |
| Live Ball | 6 | II | | 26 |
| Putting in Play | 6 | I | | 24 |
| Restrictions | 6 | VII | | 27 |
| Starting of Games & Overtime(s) | 6 | I | a | 24 |
| Starting of 2nd, 3rd & 4th Periods | 6 | I | b | 24 |
| BASKET INTERFERENCE | 11 | I | | 38 |
| **BASKET RING, BACKBOARD, SUPPORT** | | | | |
| Definition | 4 | I | | 17 |
| Hanging (Intentional) | 12A | IV | | 40 |
| Hanging (Prevent Injury) | 12A | IV | b EXCEPTION | 40 |
| CAPTAIN, DUTIES | 3 | III | | 15 |
| **CLOCK (GAME)** | | | | |
| Expiration of Time (Horn) | 2 | VIII | f | 14 |
| Expiration of Time (No Horn) | 2 | VIII | g | 14 |
| Starting—Jump Ball | 2 | VIII | b | 14 |
| | 5 | IX | d | 24 |
| Starting—Missed Free Throw | 5 | IX | b | 24 |
| Starting—Throw-in | 5 | IX | c | 24 |
| Stopping—Last Minute | 5 | V | b(1) | 21 |
| Stopping—Last Two (2) Minutes | 5 | V | b(2) | 21 |
| **CLOTHING** | | | | |
| Adjusting | 5 | V | c | 21 |
| Shirts, Tucked-In | COMMENTS ON RULES H-4 | | | 53 |
| **COACH** | | | | |
| Attire | COMMENTS ON RULES H-3 | | | 53 |
| Bench | 3 | IV | d | 15 |
| Box | 3 | IV | a | 15 |
| Conduct | 12A | V | | 40 |
| | 12A | VII | f | 43 |
| Ejection | 3 | IV | e | 15 |
| | 12A | VII | b | 42 |
| Playing Coach | 3 | IV | b | 15 |
| Speaking to Officials—Before Start of Game or Periods | 2 | II | g | 10 |
| Suspension | COMMENTS ON RULES E | | | 53 |
| CLUB PERSONNEL | 3 | IV | c | 15 |
| **CONDUCT—TEAM** | | | | |
| National Anthem | COMMENTS ON RULES H-2 | | | 54 |
| CORRECTING ERRORS | 2 | VI | | 11 |
| **COURT** | | | | |
| Dimensions, Markings | 1 | I | | 9 |
| Diagram | | | | 8 |
| DEAD BALL | 6 | IV | a | 26 |
| DEFENSIVE THREE-SECONDS | 10 | VII | | 35 |

|  | RULE | SECTION | ARTICLE | PAGE |
|---|---|---|---|---|
| **DEFINITIONS** | | | | |
| Backboard | 4 | I | | 17 |
| Basket—Choice of | 4 | I | a | 17 |
| Blocking | 4 | II | | 17 |
| Dribble | 4 | III | | 17 |
| Fouls (All Types) | 4 | IV | | 17 |
| Free Throw | 4 | V | | 18 |
| Frontcourt/Backcourt | 4 | VI | | 18 |
| Held Ball | 4 | VII | | 18 |
| Last Two Minutes | 4 | XIII | | 19 |
| Legal Goal | 5 | I | a | 20 |
| Pivot | 4 | VIII | | 18 |
| Screen | 4 | X | | 19 |
| Throw-In | 4 | XII | | 19 |
| Traveling | 4 | IX | | 19 |
| Try for Goal | 4 | XI | | 19 |
| **DELAY OF GAME** | 12A | II | | 39 |
| **DOUBLEHEADERS** | | | | |
| Neutral Court & Doubleheaders | 3 | VI | c | 16 |
| **EIGHT-SECOND BACKCOURT** | 10 | VIII | | 36 |
| **END OF PERIOD** | 5 | III | a | 21 |
| **EQUIPMENT (GAME)** | 1 | II | | 9 |
| **FIELD GOAL** | | | | |
| Two (2) Points | 5 | I | b | 20 |
| Three (3) Points | 5 | I | c | 20 |
| Opponents Basket | 5 | I | d & e | 20 |
| **FINES** | 12A | VII | | 42 |
| **FOULS (PERSONAL)** | | | | |
| Away-From-Play | 12B | X | | 48 |
| Clear-Path-To-The-Basket | 12B | I | e(6) | 44 |
| Double | 12B | VI | | 46 |
| Elbow | 12B | I | e(7) | 44 |
| Flagrant | | COMMENTS ON RULES B | | 51 |
|  | 12B | IV | | 45 |
| Loose Ball | 12B | VIII | | 47 |
| Offensive | 12B | VII | | 47 |
| Punching | 12B | IX | | 47 |
| **FOULS (TECHNICAL & OTHERS)** | | | | |
| Delay of Game—Player & Team | 12A | II | | 39 |
| Elbow—Dead Ball | 12A | V | q | 42 |
| Excessive Timeout | 12A | I | | 38 |
| Face (Eye) Guarding | 12A | V | m | 41 |
| Fighting | 12A | VI | | 42 |
| Hanging on Rim (Deliberate) | 12A | IV | a | 40 |
| Illegal Substitute | 12A | V | c | 40 |
| Maximum | 12A | V | b | 40 |
| Minimum | 12A | V | k | 41 |
| Reports | 12A | V | f | 41 |
| Throwing Ball at Official | 12A | V | p | 41 |
| Unsportsmanlike Conduct (Elbow, punching) | 12A | V | q | 42 |

|  | RULE | SECTION | ARTICLE | PAGE |
|---|---|---|---|---|
| **FREE THROW** | | | | |
| Clock, start—Unsuccessful Free Throw | 5 | IX | b | 24 |
| Clock, start—Successful Free Throw | 5 | IX | c | 24 |
| Ejection/Injured Player | 9 | II a EXCEPTION (1) | | 33 |
| Injured Player Unsportsmanlike | | II a EXCEPTION (2) | | 33 |
| Next Play | 9 | IV | | 33 |
| Penalty Situation | 12B | V | | 46 |
| Time Limit | 9 | III | | 33 |
| Technical Foul—Player Position | 9 | I | e | 32 |
| Technical Foul—Shooter | 12A | V | j | 41 |
| Technical Foul—Team Possession | 12A | V | h | 41 |
| Violations | 9 | I | | 30 |
| **GAME CANCELLATION** | | COMMENTS ON RULES D | | 53 |
| **GOALTENDING** | 11 | I | | 38 |
| **HAND-CHECKING** | 12B | I | b | 43 |
| **HOME UNIFORM** | 3 | VI | | 16 |
| **INADVERTENT WHISTLE** | 2 | V | d | 11 |
| **INSTANT REPLAY** | 13 | | | 49 |
| **JUMP BALLS** | | | | |
| Center Circle | 6 | V | | 26 |
| Double Foul—No Control | 6 | V | a (4) | 26 |
| —Held Ball, Others | 6 | VI | a | 27 |
| Illegal Tap | 6 | VII | | 27 |
| Restrictions | 6 | VII | | 27 |
| Start of Game/Overtime(s) | 6 | I | a | 24 |
| Violations | 10 | V | | 35 |
| **KICKING BALL—INTENTIONAL** | 10 | IV | b | 34 |
| **LIVE BALL** | 6 | II | | 26 |
| **OFFENSIVE FOUL** | 12B | VII | | 47 |
| **OFFENSIVE THREE SECONDS** | 10 | VI | | 35 |
| **OFFICIALS** | | | | |
| Correcting Errors | 2 | VI | | 11 |
| Designation | 2 | I | a | 10 |
| Different Decisions—On Rules | 2 | IV | a | 11 |
| Different Decisions—Out-of-Bounds | 6 | VI | a (3) | 27 |
| | 8 | II | d | 29 |
| | 2 | IV | b | 11 |
| Discussion, Coaches | 2 | II | g | 10 |
| Duties | 2 | II | | 10 |
| Elastic Power | 2 | III | | 11 |
| In Charge | 2 | II | f | 10 |
| Pre-Game Meeting | 2 | II | j | 11 |
| Reporting on Floor | 2 | II | i | 10 |
| Report on Atypical Situations | 2 | II | k | 11 |
| Time & Place for Decisions | 2 | V | | 11 |
| **OVERTIMES (TIE SCORE)** | 5 | IV | | 21 |
| **OUT-OF-BOUNDS/THROW-IN** | | | | |
| Player—Out-of-Bounds | 8 | I | | 29 |
| Ball—Out-of-Bounds | 8 | II | | 29 |

|  | RULE | SECTION | ARTICLE | PAGE |
|---|---|---|---|---|
| Designated Thrower-In | 8 | II | e | 29 |
| Throw-In Spot | 8 | III |  | 30 |
| Violations—Penalty | 10 | I |  | 33 |
| **PERSONAL FOUL** |  |  |  |  |
| Types | 12B | I |  | 43 |
| Hand-Checking | 12B | I | b | 43 |
| Dribbler | 12B | II |  | 44 |
| Screening | 12B | III |  | 45 |
| Flagrant | 12B | IV |  | 45 |
| Penalties—Free Throws | 12B | V |  | 46 |
| Double Fouls | 12B | VI |  | 46 |
| Offensive Fouls | 12B | VII |  | 47 |
| Loose Ball Fouls | 12B | VIII |  | 47 |
| Punching Fouls | 12B | IX |  | 47 |
| Away-From-Play Fouls | 12B | X |  | 48 |
| **PLAYER** |  |  |  |  |
| Conduct | 12A | V |  | 40 |
|  | COMMENTS ON RULES H |  |  | 53 |
| Conduct—Halftime & End of Game | 12A | IX | f | 43 |
| Conduct—Spectators | COMMENTS ON RULES J |  |  | 54 |
| Cursing | 12A | V | e | 40 |
| Disconcerting Free Thrower | 9 | I | f | 32 |
| Ejected | 12A | V | b | 40 |
| Failure to Report | 12A | III | d | 39 |
| Faking Free Throw | 9 | I | c | 31 |
| Equipment | 2 | II | b,c,d,e | 10 |
| Fighting | 12A | VI |  | 42 |
| Hanging on Rim (Game) | 12A | IV |  | 40 |
| Hanging on Rim (Prevent Injury) | 12A | IV | b EXCEPTION | 40 |
| Hanging on Rim (Warm-Ups) | 12A | VII | g | 43 |
| Numbering | 3 | VI | a, b | 16 |
| Proper Number on Floor | 12A | III | d | 39 |
| Shattering Backboard | COMMENTS ON RULES G |  |  | 53 |
| Suspension—Physical Contact with Official | COMMENTS ON RULES E |  |  | 53 |
| Wearing of Jewelry | 2 | II | b | 10 |
| **PROTEST** | COMMENTS ON RULES F |  |  | 53 |
| **RESTRICTED AREA NEAR BASKET** | COMMENTS ON RULES C |  |  | 52 |
| **SCORERS, DUTIES OF** | 2 | VII |  | 13 |
| **SCORING** |  |  |  |  |
| Discrepancy | 5 | I | h | 20 |
| Free Throw | 5 | I | f | 20 |
| Legal Goal | 5 | I | a | 20 |
| Tap-In—Missed Free Throw | 5 | I | g | 20 |
| Three-Point Field Goal | 5 | I | c | 20 |
| Two-Point Field Goal | 5 | I | b | 20 |
| **STARTING LINE-UPS** | 3 | II |  | 15 |
| **STRIKING THE BALL** | 10 | IV |  | 34 |
| **SUBSTITUTES** | 3 | V |  | 15 |
| **SUBSTITUTIONS** | 12A | III |  | 39 |
| **TAUNTING** | COMMENTS ON RULES P |  |  | 56 |

|  | RULE | SECTION | ARTICLE | PAGE |
|---|---|---|---|---|
| **TEAM** | | | | |
| Number of Players, Maximum & Minimum | 3 | I | | 14 |
| **TECHNICAL FOULS** | 12A | | | 38 |
| **TIMEOUT RULES** | | | | |
| After a Score | 5 | VII | | 23 |
| Backcourt—Last 2 Minutes | 5 | VII | e | 23 |
| Excessive | 12A | I | | 38 |
| Mandatory | 5 | VII | d | 23 |
| Game, Number of | 5 | VII | a | 22 |
| Last Period | 5 | VII | a | 23 |
| Options—Last 2 Minutes | 5 | VII | e | 23 |
| Out-of-bounds | 5 | VIII | e | 23 |
| Overtimes, Number of | 5 | VII | c | 23 |
| Regular | 5 | VII | | 23 |
| Twenty-Second | 5 | VI | | 21 |
| **TIME-IN** | 5 | IX | | 24 |
| **TIMERS, DUTIES OF** | 2 | VIII | | 13 |
| **TIMING (LENGTH)** | | | | |
| Between Halves | 5 | II | c | 20 |
| Disqualification | 5 | II | e | 20 |
| Overtime | 5 | II | b | 20 |
| Periods | 5 | II | a | 20 |
| **TIMING REGULATIONS** | | | | |
| End of Period | 5 | III | | 21 |
| Illegal Tap | 10 | V | | 35 |
| Public Address Announcement | 5 | II | g | 20 |
| Tie Score—Overtime | 5 | IV | | 21 |
| Time-In | 5 | IX | | 24 |
| Timeout—Regular | 5 | VII | | 22 |
| Timeout—Regular—Last 2 Minutes | 5 | II | f | 21 |
| | 5 | VII | e | 23 |
| **TWENTY-FOUR (24) SECOND CLOCK** | | | | |
| Expiration | 7 | II | k | 28 |
| Inadvertent Whistle | 7 | II | i | 28 |
| Resetting | 7 | IV | | 28 |
| Starting and Stopping | 7 | II | | 27 |
| Team Possession | 7 | II | e | 28 |
| Technical Foul | 7 | IV | d(3) | 29 |
| **UNIFORMS** | | | | |
| Number | 3 | VI | a, b | 16 |
| Color | 3 | VI | c | 16 |
| Shirts, Tucked In | COMMENTS ON RULES H-4 | | | 54 |
| Introduction | COMMENTS ON RULES H-1 | | | 54 |
| **VIOLATIONS** | | | | |
| Backcourt | 10 | IX | | 36 |
| Boundary | 10 | II | b | 34 |
| Defensive Three Seconds | 10 | VII | | 35 |
| Designated Thrower-In | 10 | III | b | 34 |
| Dribble | 10 | II | | 34 |
| Eight (8) Seconds | 10 | VIII | | 36 |

|  | RULE | SECTION | ARTICLE | PAGE |
|---|---|---|---|---|
| Entering Basket from Below | 10 | XI | | 36 |
| Five-Second Back-to-the-Basket | 10 | XV | | 37 |
| Illegal Assist in Scoring | 10 | XII | | 36 |
| Jump Ball | 10 | V | | 35 |
| Offensive Screen Out-of-Bounds | 10 | XIV | | 37 |
| Offensive Three Seconds | 10 | VI | | 35 |
| Out-of-Bounds | 10 | I | | 33 |
| Run With the Ball | 10 | II | a | 34 |
| Striking the Ball—Leg, Foot or Fist | 10 | IV | | 34 |
| Swinging of Elbows | 10 | X | | 36 |
| Thrower-In | 10 | III | | 34 |
| Throw-In | 8 | III | | 30 |
| Traveling | 10 | XIII | | 37 |

# OFFICIAL NBA COURT DIAGRAM

# Official Rules

### RULE NO. 1—COURT DIMENSIONS—EQUIPMENT

#### Section I—Court and Dimensions

a. The playing court shall be measured and marked as shown in the court diagram. (See page 8)

b. A free throw lane shall be marked at each end of the court with dimensions and markings as shown on the court diagram. All boundary lines are part of the lane; lane space marks and neutral zone marks are not. The color of the lane space marks and neutral zones shall contrast with the color of the boundary lines. The areas identified by the lane space markings are 2" by 8" inches and the neutral zone marks are 12" by 8".

c. A free throw line shall be drawn (2" wide) across each of the circles indicated in the court diagram. It shall be parallel to the end line and shall be 15' from the plane of the face of the backboard.

d. The three-point field goal area has parallel lines 3' from the sidelines, extending from the baseline and an arc of 23'9" from the middle of the basket which intersects the parallel lines.

e. Four hash marks shall be drawn (2" wide) perpendicular to the sideline on each side of the court and 28' from the baseline. These hash marks shall extend 3' onto the court.

f. Four hash marks shall be drawn (2" wide) perpendicular to the baseline on each side of the free throw lane line. These hash marks shall be 3' from the free throw lane line and extend 6" onto the court.

g. Four hash marks shall be drawn (2" wide) parallel to the baseline on each side of the free throw circle. These hash marks shall be 13' from the baseline and 3' from the free throw lane lines and shall be 6" in length.

h. Two hash marks shall be drawn (2" wide) perpendicular to the sideline, in front of the scorer's table, and 4' on each side of the midcourt line. This will designate the Substitution Box area.

i. A half-circle shall be created 4' from the center of the basket with a solid two-inch line.

#### Section II—Equipment

a. The backboard shall be a rectangle measuring 6' horizontally and $3\,^1/_2$' vertically. The front surface shall be flat and transparent.

b. A transparent backboard shall be marked with a 2" white rectangle centered behind the ring. This rectangle shall have outside dimensions of 24" horizontally and 18" vertically.

c. Home management is required to have a spare board with supporting unit on hand for emergencies, and a steel tape or extension ruler and a level for use if necessary.

d. Each basket shall consist of a pressure-release NBA approved metal safety ring 18" in inside diameter with a white cord net 15" to 18" in length. The cord of the net shall not be less than 30 thread nor more than 120 thread and shall be constructed to check the ball momentarily as it passes through the basket.

e. Each basket ring shall be securely attached to the backboard with its upper edge 10' above and parallel to the floor and equidistant from the vertical edges of the board. The nearest point of the inside edge of the ring shall be 6" from the plane of the face of the board. The ring shall be painted orange.

f. (1) The ball shall be an officially approved NBA ball between $7\frac{1}{2}$ and $8\frac{1}{2}$ pounds pressure.

(2) Six balls must be made available to each team for pre-game warmup.

g. At least one electric light is to be placed behind the backboard, obvious to officials and synchronized to light up when the horn sounds at the expiration of time for each period. The electric light is to be "red."

## RULE NO. 2—OFFICIALS AND THEIR DUTIES

### Section I—The Game Officials

a. The game officials shall be a crew chief and two referees. They will be assisted by an official scorer and two trained timers. One timer will operate the game clock and the other will operate the 24-second clock. All officials shall be approved by the Basketball Operations Department.

b. The officials shall wear the uniform prescribed by the NBA.

### Section II—Duties of the Officials

a. The officials shall, prior to the start of the game, inspect and approve all equipment, including court, baskets, balls, backboards, timer's and scorer's equipment.

b. The officials shall not permit players to play with any type of hand, arm, face, nose, ear, head or neck jewelry.

c. The officials shall not permit any player to wear equipment which, in their judgment, is dangerous to other players. Any equipment which is of hard substance (casts, splints, guards and braces) must be padded or foam covered and have no exposed sharp or cutting edge. All the face masks and eye or nose protectors must conform to the contour of the face and have no sharp or protruding edges. Approval is on a game-to-game basis.

d. All equipment used must be appropriate for basketball. Equipment that is unnatural and designed to increase a player's height or reach, or to gain an advantage, shall not be used.

e. The officials must check the game ball to see that it is properly inflated. The recommended ball pressure should be between $7\frac{1}{2}$ and $8\frac{1}{2}$ pounds.

f. The crew chief shall be the official in charge.

g. If a coach desires to discuss a rule or interpretation of a rule prior to the start of a game or between periods, it will be mandatory for the officials to ask the other coach to be present during the discussion. The same procedure shall be followed if the officials wish to discuss a game situation with either coach.

h. The designated official shall toss the ball at the start of the game. The crew chief shall decide whether or not a goal shall count if the officials disagree, and he shall decide matters upon which scorers and timers disagree.

i. All officials shall be present during the 20-minute pre-game warm-up period to observe and report to the Basketball Operations Department any infractions of Rule 12A-Section IX—j (hanging on the basket ring) and to review scoring and timing procedures with table personnel. Officials may await the on-court arrival of the first team.

j. Officials must meet with team captains prior to the start of the game.

k. Officials must report any atypical or unique incident to the Basketball Operations Department by E-mail. Flagrant, punching, fighting fouls or a team's failure to have eight players to begin the game must also be reported.

## Section III—Elastic Power

The officials shall have the power to make decisions on any point not specifically covered in the rules. The Basketball Operations Department will be advised of all such decisions at the earliest possible moment.

## Section IV—Different Decisions By Officials

a. The crew chief shall have the authority to set aside or question decisions regarding a rule interpretation made by either of the other officials.

b. If the officials give conflicting signals as to who caused the ball to go out-of-bounds, a jump ball shall be called between the two players involved. However, if an official offers assistance, the calling official may change the call.

c. In the event that a violation and foul occur at the same time, the foul will take precedence.

d. Double Foul (See Rule 12-B—Section VI-f).

## Section V—Time and Place for Decisions

a. The officials have the power to render decisions for infractions of rules committed inside or outside the boundary lines. This includes periods when the game may be stopped for any reason.

b. When a personal foul or violation occurs, an official will blow his whistle to terminate play. The whistle is the signal for the timer to stop the game clock. If a personal foul has occurred, the official will indicate the number of the offender to the official scorer, the type of foul committed and the number of free throws, if any, to be attempted or indicate the spot of the throw-in.

If a violation has occurred the official will indicate (1) the nature of the violation by giving the correct signal (2) the number of the offender, if applicable (3) the direction in which the ball will be advanced.

c. When a team is entitled to a throw-in, an official shall clearly signal (1) the act which caused the ball to become dead (2) the spot of the throw-in (3) the team entitled to the throw-in, unless it follows a successful field goal or free throw.

d. When a whistle is erroneously sounded, whether the ball is in a possession or non-possession status, it is an inadvertent whistle and shall be interpreted as a suspension-of-play.

e. An official may suspend play for any unusual circumstance (Rule 4-Section XV).

## Section VI—Correcting Errors

A. FREE THROWS

Officials may correct an error if a rule is inadvertently set aside and results in the following:

(1) A team not shooting a merited free throw that will remain in play.

EXCEPTION: If the offensive team scores or shoots earned free throws as a result of a personal foul prior to possession by the defensive team the error shall be ignored if more than 24 seconds has expired.

(2) A team not shooting a merited free throw that will not remain in play. The error shall be corrected, all play shall stand and play will resume from the point of interruption with the clocks remaining the same.

(3) A team shooting an unmerited free throw.

(4) Permitting the wrong player to attempt a free throw.

a. Officials shall be notified of a possible error at the first dead ball.

b. Errors which occur in the first or third periods must be discovered and rectified prior to the start of the next period.

c. Errors which occur in the second period must be discovered and the scorer's table notified prior to the officials leaving the floor at the end of the period. The error(s) must be rectified prior to the start of the third period.

d. Errors which occur in the fourth period or overtime(s) must be discovered and rectified prior to the end of the period.

e. The ball is not in play on corrected free throw attempt(s). Play is resumed at the same spot and under the same conditions as would have prevailed had the error not been discovered.

f. All play that occurs is to be nullified if the error is discovered within a 24-second time period. The game clock shall be reset to the time that the error occurred.

EXCEPTION (1): Acts of unsportsmanlike conduct and all flagrant fouls, and points scored therefrom, shall not be nullified.

EXCEPTION (2): If the error to be corrected is for a free throw attempt where there is to be no line-up of players on the free throw lane (technical foul, defensive three seconds, flagrant foul, clear path-to-the-basket foul, punching foul, away-from-the-play foul in last two minutes) the error shall be corrected, all play shall stand and play shall resume from the point of interruption with the clocks remaining the same.

## B. LINEUP POSITIONS

In any jump ball situation, if the jumpers lined up incorrectly, and the error is discovered:

(1) After more than 24 seconds has elapsed, the teams will continue to shoot for that basket for the remainder of that half and/or overtime. If the error is discovered in the first half, teams will shoot at the proper basket as decided by the opening tap for the second half.

(2) If 24 seconds or less has elapsed, all play shall be nullified.

EXCEPTION: Acts of unsportsmanlike conduct, all flagrant fouls, and points scored therefrom, shall not be nullified and play will resume from the original jump ball with players facing the proper direction.

## C. START OF PERIOD—POSSESSION

If the second, third or fourth period begins with the wrong team being awarded possession, and the error is discovered:

(1) after 24 seconds has elapsed, the error cannot be corrected.

(2) with 24 seconds or less having elapsed, all play shall be nullified.

EXCEPTION: Acts of unsportsmanlike conduct, all flagrant fouls, and points scored therefrom, shall not be nullified.

## D. RECORD KEEPING

A record keeping error by the official scorer which involves the score, number of personal fouls and/or timeouts may be corrected by the officials at any time prior to the end of the fourth period. Any such error which occurs in overtime must be corrected prior to the end of that period.

### Section VII—Duties of Scorers

a. The scorers shall record the field goals made, the free throws made and missed and shall keep a running summary of the points scored. They shall record the personal and technical fouls called on each player and shall notify the officials immediately when a sixth personal foul is called on any player. They shall record the timeouts charged to each team, shall notify a team and its coach through an official whenever that team takes a sixth charged timeout and shall notify the nearest official each time a team is granted a charged timeout in excess of the legal number. In case there is a question about an error in the scoring, the scorer shall check with the crew chief at once to find the discrepancy. If the error cannot be found, the official shall accept the record of the official scorer, unless he has knowledge that forces him to decide otherwise.

b. The scorers shall keep a record of the names, numbers and positions of the players who are to start the game and of all substitutes who enter the game. When there is an infraction of the rules pertaining to submission of the lineup, substitutions or numbers of players, they shall notify the nearest official immediately if the ball is dead, or as soon as it becomes dead if it is in play when the infraction is discovered. The scorer shall mark the time at which players are disqualified by reason of receiving six personal fouls, so that it may be easy to ascertain the order in which the players are eligible to go back into the game in accordance with Rule 3—Section I.

c. The scorers shall use a horn or other device unlike that used by the officials or timers to signal the officials. This may be used when the ball is dead or in certain specified situations when the ball is in control of a given team.

d. When a player is disqualified from the game, or whenever a penalty free throw is being awarded, a buzzer, siren or some other clearly audible sound must be used by the scorer or timer to notify the game officials. It is the duty of the scorekeeper to be certain the officials have acknowledged the sixth personal foul buzzer and the penalty shot buzzer.

e. The scorer shall not signal the officials while the ball is in play, except to notify them of the necessity to correct an error.

f. Should the scorer sound the horn while the ball is in play, it shall be ignored by the players on the court. The officials must use their judgment in stopping play to consult with the scorer's table.

g. Scorers shall record on the scoreboard the number of team fouls up to a total of five, which will indicate that the team is in a penalty situation.

h. Scorers shall, immediately, record the name of the team which secures the first possession of the game.

### Section VIII—Duties of Timers

a. The timers shall note when each half is to start and shall notify the crew chief and both coaches five minutes before this time, or cause them to be notified at least five minutes before the half is to start. They shall signal the scorers two minutes before starting time. They shall record playing time and time of stoppages as provided in the rules. The official timer and the 24-second clock operator shall be provided with digital stop watches to be used with the timing of timeouts and in case the official game clock, 24-second clocks/game clocks located above the backboards fail to work properly.

b. At the beginning of the first period, any overtime period or whenever play is resumed by a jump ball, the game clock shall be started when the ball is legally tapped by either of the jumpers. No time will be removed from the game clock and/or 24-second clock if there is an illegal tap.

c. If the game clock has been stopped for a violation, successful field goal or free throw attempt and the ball is put in play by a throw-in, the game clock and the 24-second clock shall be started when the ball is legally touched by any player on the court. The starting of the game clock and the 24-second clock will be under the control of the official timer.

d. During an unsuccessful free throw attempt, the game clock will be started when the ball is legally touched. The 24-second clock will be reset when player possession of the ball is obtained.

e. The game clock shall be stopped at the expiration of time for each period and when an official signals timeout. For a charged timeout, the timer shall start a digital stop watch and shall signal the official when it is time to resume play.

f. The game clock and the scoreboard will combine to cause a horn to sound, automatically, when playing time for the period has expired. If the horn or buzzer fails to sound, or is not heard, the official timer shall use any other means to notify the officials immediately.

g. In a dead ball situation, if the clock shows :00.0, the period or game is considered to have ended although the horn may not have sounded.

EXCEPTION: See Rule 13—II—a(6)

h. Record only the actual playing time in the last minute of the first, second and third periods.

i. Record only the actual playing time in the last two minutes of the fourth period and the last two minutes of any overtime period(s).

## RULE NO. 3—PLAYERS, SUBSTITUTES AND COACHES

### Section I—Team

a. Each team shall consist of five players. No team may be reduced to less than five players. If a player in the game receives his sixth personal foul and all substitutes have already been disqualified, said player shall remain in the game and shall be charged with a personal and team foul. A technical foul also shall be assessed against his team. All subsequent personal fouls, including offensive fouls, shall be treated similarly. All players who have six or more personal fouls and remain in the game shall be treated similarly.

b. In the event that there are only five eligible players remaining and one of these players is injured and must leave the game or is ejected, he must be replaced by the last player who was disqualified by reason of receiving six personal fouls. Each subsequent requirement to replace an injured or ejected player will be treated in this inverse order. Any such re-entry into a game by a disqualified player shall be penalized by a technical foul.

c. In the event that a player becomes ill and must leave the court while the ball is in play, the official will stop play immediately when his team gains new possession. The player shall be replaced and no technical foul will be assessed. The opposing team is also permitted to substitute one player.

### Section II—Starting Line-Ups

At least ten minutes before the game is scheduled to begin, the scorers shall be supplied with the name and number of each player who may participate in the game. Starting line-ups will be indicated. Failure to comply with this provision shall be reported to the Basketball Operations Department.

### Section III—The Captain

a. A team may have a captain and a co-captain numbering a maximum of two. The designated captain may be anyone on the squad who is in uniform, except a player-coach.

b. The designated captain is the only player who may ask an official about a rule interpretation during a regular or 20-second timeout charged to his team. He may not discuss a judgment decision.

c. If the designated captain continues to sit on the bench, he remains the captain for the entire game.

d. In the event that the captain is absent from the court and bench, his coach shall immediately designate a new captain.

### Section IV—The Coach and Others

a. The coach's position may be on or off the bench from the 28' hash mark to the baseline. They are permitted between the 28' hash mark and the midcourt line to relay information to players but must return to the bench side of the 28' hash mark immediately or be called for a non-unsportsmanlike technical foul. A coach is not permitted to cross the midcourt line and violators will be assessed an unsportsmanlike technical foul immediately. All assistants and trainers must remain on the bench. Coaches and trainers are not permitted to go to the scorer's table, for any reason, except during a dead ball.

b. A player-coach will have no special privileges. He is to conduct himself in the same manner as any other player.

c. Any club personnel not seated on the bench must conduct themselves in a manner that would reflect favorably on the dignity of the game or that of the officials. Violations by any of the personnel indicated shall require a written report to the Basketball Operations Department for subsequent action.

d. The bench shall be occupied only by a league-approved head coach, a maximum of three assistant coaches, players and trainer. During an altercation, the head and assistant coaches are permitted on the court as 'peacemakers.'

e. If a player, coach or assistant coach is suspended from a game or games, he shall not at any time before, during or after such game or games appear in any part of the arena or stands where his team is playing. A player, coach or assistant coach who is ejected may only remain in the dressing room of his team during the remainder of the game, or leave the building. A violation of this rule shall call for an automatic fine of $500.

### Section V—Substitutes

a. A substitute shall report to the scorer and position himself in the 8' Substitution Box located in front of the scorer's table. He shall inform the scorer whom he is going to replace. The scorer shall sound the horn as soon as the ball is dead to indicate a substitution. The horn does not have to be sounded if the substitution occurs between periods or during timeouts. No substitute may enter the game after a successful field goal by either team, unless the ball is dead due to a personal foul, technical foul, timeout or violation. He may enter the game after the first of multiple free throws, whether made or missed.

b. The substitute shall remain in the Substitution Box until he is beckoned onto the court by an official. If the ball is about to become live, the beckoning signal shall be withheld. Any player who enters the court prior to being beckoned by an official shall be assessed a non-unsportsmanlike technical foul.

c. A substitute must be ready to enter the game when beckoned. No delays for removal of warm-up clothing will be permitted.

d. The substitute shall not replace a free throw shooter or a player involved in a jump ball unless dictated to do so by an injury, whereby he is selected by the opposing coach. At no time may he be allowed to attempt a free throw awarded as a result of a technical foul.

e. A substitute shall be considered as being in the game when he is beckoned onto the court or recognized as being in the game by an official. Once a player is in the game, he cannot be removed until the ball is legally touched by a player on the court unless: (1) a personal or technical foul is called, (2) there is a change of possession or (3) administration of infection control rule.

f. A substitute may be recalled from the scorer's table prior to being beckoned onto the court by an official.

g. A player may be replaced and allowed to re-enter the game as a substitute during the same dead ball.

h. A player must be in the Substitution Box at the time a violation occurs if the throw-in is to be administered in the backcourt. If a substitute fails to meet this requirement, he may not enter the game until the next legal opportunity.

EXCEPTION: In the last two minutes of each period or overtime, a reasonable amount of time will be allowed for a substitution.

i. Notification of all above infractions and ensuing procedures shall be in accordance with Rule 2—Section VII.

j. No substitutes are allowed to enter the game during an official's suspension-of-play for (1) a delay-of-game warning, (2) retrieving an errant ball (3) an inadvertent whistle or (4) any other unusual circumstance.

EXCEPTION: Suspension of play for a player bleeding. See Comments on the Rules—N.

### Section VI—Uniforms (Players Jerseys)

a. Each player shall be numbered on the front and back of his jersey with a number of solid color contrasting with the color of the shirt.

b. Each number must be not less than $3/4$" in width and not less than 6" in height on both the front and back. Each player shall have his surname affixed to the back of his game jersey in letters at least 2" in height.

c. The home team shall wear light color jerseys, and the visitors dark jerseys. For neutral court games and doubleheaders, the second team named in the official schedule shall be regarded as the home team and shall wear the light colored jerseys.

# RULE NO. 4—DEFINITIONS

## Section I—Basket/Backboard

a. A team's basket consists of the basket ring and net through which its players try to shoot the ball. The visiting team has the choice of baskets for the first half. The basket selected by the visiting team when it first enters onto the court shall be its basket for the first half.

b. The teams change baskets for the second half. All overtime periods are considered extensions of the second half.

c. Five sides of the backboard (front, two sides, bottom and top) are considered in play when contacted by the basketball. The back of the backboard and the area directly behind it are out-of-bounds.

## Section II—Blocking

Blocking is illegal personal contact which impedes the progress of an opponent.

## Section III—Dribble

A dribble is movement of the ball, caused by a player in control, who throws or taps the ball to the floor.

a. The dribble ends when the dribbler:

(1) Touches the ball simultaneously with both hands
(2) Permits the ball to come to rest while he is in control of it
(3) Tries for a field goal
(4) Throws a pass
(5) Touches the ball more than once while dribbling, before it touches the floor
(6) Loses control
(7) Allows the ball to become dead

## Section IV—Fouls

a. A common personal foul is illegal physical contact which occurs with an opponent after the ball has become live or before the horn sounds to end the period. If time expires before the personal foul occurs, the personal foul should be disregarded, unless it was unsportsmanlike.

EXCEPTION: If the foul is committed on or by a player in the act of shooting, and the shooter released the ball prior to the expiration of time on the game clock, then the foul should be administered in the same manner as with any similar play during the course of the game (See Rule 13—Section II—a(6).)

b. A technical foul is the penalty for unsportsmanlike conduct or violations by team members on the floor or seated on the bench. It may be assessed for illegal contact which occurs with an opponent before the ball becomes live.

c. A double foul is a situation in which any two opponents commit personal fouls at approximately the same time.

d. An offensive foul is illegal contact, committed by an offensive player, after the ball is live.

e. A loose ball foul is illegal contact, after the ball is alive, when team control does not exist.

f. An elbow foul is making contact with the elbow in an unsportsmanlike manner whether the ball is dead or alive.

g. A flagrant foul is unnecessary and/or excessive contact committed by a player against an opponent whether the ball is dead or alive.

h. A punching foul is a punch by a player which makes contact with an opponent whether the ball is dead or alive.

i. An away-from-the-play foul is illegal contact by the defense in the last two minutes of the game, and/or overtime, which occurs (1) deliberately away from the immediate area of offensive action, and/or (2) prior to the ball being released on a throw-in.

### Section V—Free Throw

A free throw is the privilege given a player to score one point by an unhindered attempt for the goal from a position directly behind the free throw line. This attempt must be made within 10 seconds.

### Section VI—Frontcourt/Backcourt

a. A team's frontcourt consists of that part of the court between its endline and the nearer edge of the midcourt line, including the basket and inbounds part of the backboard.

b. A team's backcourt consists of the entire midcourt line and the rest of the court to include the opponent's basket and inbounds part of the backboard.

c. A ball being held by a player: (1) is in the frontcourt if neither the ball nor the player is touching the backcourt, (2) is in the backcourt if either the ball or player is touching the backcourt.

d. A ball being dribbled is (1) in the frontcourt when the ball and both feet of the player are in the frontcourt, (2) in the backcourt if the ball or either foot of the player is in the backcourt.

e. The ball is considered in the frontcourt once it has broken the plane of the midcourt line and is not in player control.

f. The team on offense must bring the ball across the midcourt line within 8 seconds.

EXCEPTION: (1) kicked ball, (2) punched ball, (3) personal or technical foul on the defensive team, (4) delay-of-game warning on the defensive team or (5) infection control.

g. Frontcourt/backcourt status is not attained until a player with the ball has established a positive position in either half during (1) a jump ball, (2) a steal by a defensive player, (3) a throw-in in the last two minutes of the fourth period and/or any overtime period or (4) any time the ball is loose.

### Section VII—Held Ball

A held ball occurs when two opponents have one or both hands firmly on the ball or anytime a defensive player touches the ball causing the offensive player to return to the floor with the ball in his continuous possession.

A held ball should not be called until both players have hands so firmly on the ball that neither can gain sole possession without undue roughness. If a player is lying or sitting on the floor while in possession, he should have an opportunity to throw the ball, but a held ball should be called if there is danger of injury.

### Section VIII—Pivot

a. A pivot takes place when a player, who is holding the ball, steps once or more than once in any direction with the same foot, with the other foot (pivot foot) in contact with the floor.

b. If the player wishes to dribble after a pivot, the ball must be out of his hand before the pivot foot is raised off the floor. If the player raises his pivot off the floor, he must pass or attempt a field goal.

If he fails to follow these guidelines, he has committed a traveling violation.

### Section IX—Traveling

Traveling is progressing in any direction while in possession of the ball, which is in excess of prescribed limits as noted in Rule 4—Section VIII and Rule 10—Section XIV.

### Section X—Screen

A screen is the legal action of a player who, without causing undue contact, delays or prevents an opponent from reaching a desired position.

### Section XI—Field Goal Attempt

A field goal attempt is a player's attempt to shoot the ball into his basket for a field goal. The act of shooting starts when, in the official's judgment, the player has started his shooting motion and continues until the shooting motion ceases and he returns to a normal floor position. It is not essential that the ball leave the shooter's hand. His arm(s) might be held so that he cannot actually make an attempt.

The term is also used to include the flight of the ball until it becomes dead or is touched by a player. A tap during a jump ball or rebound is not considered a field goal attempt. However, anytime a live ball is in flight from the playing court, the goal, if made, shall count, even if time expires or the official's whistle sounds. The field goal will not be scored if time on the game clock expires before the ball leaves the player's hand.

### Section XII—Throw-In

A throw-in is a method of putting the ball in play from out-of-bounds in accordance with Rule 8—Section III. The throw-in begins when the ball is at the disposal of the team or player entitled to it, and ends when the ball is released by the thrower-in.

### Section XIII—Last Two Minutes

When the game clock shows 2:00, the game is considered to be in the two-minute period.

### Section XIV—Suspension of Play

An official can suspend play for retrieving an errant ball, re-setting the timing devices, delay-of-game warning, inadvertent whistle or any other unusual circumstance. During such a suspension, neither team is permitted to substitute and the defensive team may not be granted a timeout. Play shall be resumed at the point of interruption.

EXCEPTION: See Comments on Rules—N.

### Section XV—Point of Interruption

Where the ball is located when the whistle sounds.

### Section XVI—Team Control

A team is in control when a player is holding, dribbling or passing the ball. Team control ends when the defensive team deflects the ball or there is a field goal attempt.

### Section XVII—Team Possession

A team is in possession when a player is holding, dribbling or passing the ball. Team possession ends when the defensive team gains possession or there is a field goal attempt.

## RULE NO. 5—SCORING AND TIMING

### Section I—Scoring

a. A legal field goal or free throw attempt shall be scored when a live ball from the playing area enters the basket from above and remains in or passes through the net.

b. A successful field goal attempt from the area on or inside the three-point field goal line shall count two points.

c. A successful field goal attempt from the area outside the three-point field goal line shall count three points.

  (1) The shooter must have at least one foot on the floor outside the three-point field goal line prior to the attempt.
  (2) The shooter may not be touching the floor on or inside the three-point field goal line.
  (3) The shooter may contact the three-point field goal line, or land in the two-point field goal area, after the ball is released.

d. A field goal accidentally scored in an opponent's basket shall be added to the opponent's score, credited to the opposing player nearest the shooter and mentioned in a footnote.

e. It is a violation for a player to attempt a field goal at an opponent's basket. The opposing team will be awarded the ball at the free throw line extended.

f. A successful free throw attempt shall count one point.

g. An unsuccessful free throw attempt which is tapped into the basket shall count two points and shall be credited to the player who tapped the ball in.

h. If there is a discrepancy in the score and it cannot be resolved, the running score shall be official.

### Section II—Timing

a. All periods of regulation play in the NBA will be twelve minutes.

b. All overtime periods of play will be five minutes.

c. Fifteen minutes will be permitted between halves of all games.

d. 130 seconds will be permitted between the first and second periods, the third and fourth periods and before any overtime period.

e. A team is permitted a total of 30 seconds to replace a disqualified player.

f. The game is considered to be in the two-minute part when the game clock shows 2:00 or less time remaining in the period.

g. The public address operator is required to announce that there are two minutes remaining in each period.

h. The game clock shall be equipped to show tenths-of-a-second during the last minute of each period.

### Section III—End of Period

a. Each period ends when time expires.

EXCEPTIONS:

(1) If a live ball is in flight, the period ends when the goal is made, missed or touched by an offensive player.

(2) If the official's whistle sounds prior to the horn or :00.0 on the clock, the period is not over and time must be added to the clock.

(3) If the ball is in the air when the horn sounds ending a period, and it subsequently is touched by: (a) a defensive player, the goal, if successful, shall count; or (b) an offensive player, the period has ended.

(4) If a timeout request is made at approximately the instant time expires for a period, the period ends and the timeout shall not be granted.

(5) If there is a foul called on or by a player in the act of shooting the period will end after the foul is penalized. (See Rule 13—II—a[6])

b. If the ball is dead and the game clock shows :00.0, the period has ended even though the horn may not have sounded.

EXCEPTION: See Rule 13—II—a(6)

### Section IV—Tie Score—Overtime

If the score is tied at the end of the fourth period, play shall resume in 130 seconds without change of baskets for any of the overtime periods required. (See Rule 5—Section II—d for the amount of time between overtime periods.)

### Section V—Stoppage of Timing Devices

a. The timing devices shall be stopped whenever the official's whistle sounds indicating one of the following:

(1) A personal or technical foul.

(2) A jump ball.

(3) A floor violation.

(4) An unusual delay.

(5) A suspension-of-play.

(6) A regular or 20-second timeout.

b. The timing devices shall be stopped:

(1) During the last minute of the first, second and third periods following a successful field goal attempt.

(2) During the last two minutes of regulation play and/or overtime(s) following a successful field goal attempt.

c. Officials may not use official time to permit a player to change or repair equipment.

### Section VI—20-Second Timeout

A player's request for a 20-second timeout shall be granted only when the ball is dead or in control of a player on the team making the request. A request at any other time shall be ignored.

EXCEPTION: The head coach may request a 20-second timeout if there is a suspension of play to administer Comments on the Rules—N—Guidelines for Infection Control.

a. Each team is entitled to one (1) 20-second timeout per half for a total of two (2) per game, including overtimes.

b. During a 20-second timeout a team may only substitute for one player. If the team calling the 20-second timeout replaces a player, the opposing team may also replace one player.

EXCEPTION: In the last two minutes of the fourth period and/or any overtime period, free substitution is permitted by both teams.

c. If a second 20-second timeout is requested during a half (including overtimes), it shall be granted. It will automatically become a charged regular timeout. Overtimes are considered to be an extension of the second half.

d. The official shall instruct the timer to record the 20 seconds and to inform him when the time has expired. If a team calls a 20-second timeout because one of its players is injured and, at the expiration of the 20-second timeout limit, play is unable to resume due to that player's injury, a full timeout will be charged to that team and the 20-second timeout returned.

EXCEPTION: If a team does not have any full timeouts remaining, only the 20-second timeout will be charged. Play will resume when playing conditions are safe.

e. This rule may be used for any reason, including a request for a rule interpretation. If the correction is sustained, no timeout shall be charged.

f. Players should say "20-second timeout" when requesting this time.

g. If a 20-second timeout is requested by the offensive team during the last two minutes of the fourth period and/or any overtime period and (1) the ball is out-of-bounds in the backcourt (except for a suspension of play after the team had advanced the ball), or (2) after securing the ball from a rebound in the backcourt and prior to any advance of the ball, or (3) after the offensive team secures the ball from a change of possession in the backcourt and prior to any advance of the ball, the timeout should be granted. Upon resumption of play, the team granted the timeout shall have the option of putting the ball into play at the 28' hash mark in the frontcourt or at the designated spot out-of-bounds. If the ball is put into play at the hash mark, the ball may be passed into either the frontcourt or backcourt. If it is passed into the backcourt, the team will receive a new 8-second count.

h. If a 20-second timeout has been granted and a mandatory timeout by the same team is due, only the mandatory timeout will be charged.

i. A 20-second timeout shall not be granted to the defensive team during an official's suspension-of-play for (1) delay-of-game warning, (2) retrieving an errant ball, (3) an inadvertent whistle or (4) any other unusual circumstance.

EXCEPTION: Suspension of play for a player bleeding. See Comments on the Rules—N.

### Section VII—Regular Timeout—100/60 Seconds

A player's request for a timeout shall be granted only when the ball is dead or in control of a player on the team making the request. A request at any other time shall be ignored.

EXCEPTION: The head coach may request a regular timeout if there is a suspension of play to administer Comments on the Rules—N—Guidelines for Infection Control.

a. Each team is entitled to six (6) charged timeouts during regulation play. Each team is limited to no more than three (3) timeouts in the fourth period and no more than two (2) timeouts in the last two minutes of regulation play. (This is in addition to one 20-second timeout per half.)

b. During a regular timeout, both teams may have unlimited substitutions.

c. In overtime periods each team shall be allowed three (3) 60-second timeouts regardless of the number of timeouts called or remaining during regulation play or previous overtimes. Teams are permitted no more than two timeouts in the last two minutes of the period.

d. There must be two 100-second timeouts in the first and third periods and three 100-second timeouts in the second and fourth periods.

If neither team has taken a timeout prior to 5:59 of the first or third period, it shall be mandatory for the Official Scorer to take it at the first dead ball and charge it to the home team. If no subsequent timeouts are taken prior to 2:59, it shall be mandatory for the Official Scorer to take it and charge it to the team not previously charged.

If neither team has taken a timeout prior to 8:59 of the second or fourth period, a mandatory timeout will be called by the Official Scorer and charged to neither team. If there are no subsequent timeouts taken prior to 5:59, it shall be mandatory for the Official Scorer to take it at the first dead ball and charge it to the home team. If no subsequent timeouts are taken prior to 2:59, it shall be mandatory for the Official Scorer to take it and charge it to the team not previously charged.

The Official Scorer shall notify a team when it has been charged with a mandatory timeout.

Any additional timeouts in a period beyond those which are mandatory shall be 60 seconds.

No regular or mandatory timeout shall be granted to the defensive team during an official's suspension-of-play for (1) a delay-of-game warning, (2) retrieving an errant ball, (3) an inadvertent whistle, or (4) any other unusual circumstance.

EXCEPTION: Suspension-of-play for Infection Control. See Comments on the Rules—N.

e. If a regular or mandatory timeout is awarded the offensive team during the last two minutes of the fourth period and/or any overtime period and (1) the ball is out-of-bounds in the backcourt (except for a suspension of play after the team had advanced the ball), or (2) after securing the ball from a rebound in the backcourt and prior to any advance of the ball, or (3) after securing the ball from a change of possession in the backcourt and prior to any advance of the ball, the timeout shall be granted. Upon resumption of play, the team granted the timeout shall have the option of putting the ball into play at the 28' hash mark in the frontcourt, or at the designated spot out-of-bounds. If the ball is put into play at the hash mark, the ball may be passed into either the frontcourt or backcourt. If the ball is passed into the backcourt, the team will receive a new 8-second count.

However, once the ball is (1) thrown in from out-of-bounds, or (2) dribbled or passed after receiving it from a rebound or a change of possession, the timeout shall be granted, and, upon resumption of play, the ball shall be in-bounded on the sideline where play was interrupted.

The time on the game clock and the 24-second clock shall remain as when the timeout was called. In order for the option to be available under the conditions in paragraph #2 above, the offensive team must call two successive timeouts.

f. No timeout shall be charged if it is called to question a rule interpretation and the correction is sustained.

g. Requests for a timeout in excess of the authorized number shall be granted and a technical foul shall be assessed. Following the timeout, the ball will be awarded to the opposing team and play shall resume with a throw-in nearest the spot where play was interrupted. If a player is injured and cannot be removed from the playing court during a stoppage of play, no excessive timeout will be charged and play will resume when playing conditions are safe.

## Section VIII—Timeout Requests

a. If an official, upon receiving a timeout request (regular or 20-second) by the defensive team, inadvertently signals while the play is in progress, play shall be suspended and the team in possession shall put the ball in play immediately at the sideline nearest where the ball was when the signal was given. The team in possession shall have only the time remaining of the original eight seconds in which to move the ball into the frontcourt. The 24-second clock shall remain the same.

b. If an official, upon receiving a timeout request (regular or 20-second) from the defensive team, inadvertently signals for a timeout during: (1) a successful field goal or free throw attempt, the point(s) shall be scored; (2) an unsuccessful field goal attempt, play shall be resumed with a jump ball at the center circle between any two opponents; (3) an unsuccessful free throw attempt, the official shall rule disconcerting and award a substitute free throw.

c. If an official inadvertently blows his whistle during (1) a successful field goal or free throw attempt, the points shall be scored, or (2) an unsuccessful field goal or free throw attempt, play shall be resumed with a jump ball at the center circle between any two opponents.

d. When a team is granted a regular or 20-second time-out, play shall not resume until the full 100 seconds, 60 seconds, or 20 seconds have elapsed. The throw-in shall be nearest the spot where play was suspended. The throw-in shall be on the sideline, if the ball was in play when the request was granted.

e. A player shall not be granted a timeout (regular or 20-second) if both of his feet are in the air and any part of his body has broken the vertical plane of the boundary line (including the midcourt line).

## Section IX—Time-In

a. After time has been out, the game clock shall be started when the ball is legally touched by any player within the playing area of the court.

b. On a free throw that is unsuccessful and the ball continues in play, the game clock shall be started when the missed free throw is legally touched by any player.

c. If play is resumed by a throw-in from out-of-bounds, the game clock shall be started when the ball is legally touched by any player within the playing area of the court.

d. If play is resumed with a jump ball, the game clock shall be started when the ball is legally tapped.

## RULE NO. 6—PUTTING BALL IN PLAY—LIVE/DEAD BALL

## Section I—Start of Games/Periods and Others

a. The game and overtimes shall be started with a jump ball in the center circle.

b. The team which gains first possession of the game will put the ball into play at their opponent's endline to begin the fourth period. The other team will put the ball into play at their opponent's endline at the beginning of the second and third periods.

c. In putting the ball into play, the thrower-in may run along the endline or pass it to a teammate who is also out-of-bounds at the endline—as after a score.

d. After any dead ball, play shall be resumed by a jump ball, a throw-in or by placing the ball at the disposal of a free-thrower.

—24—

e. On the following infractions, the ball shall be awarded to the opposing team out-of-bounds on the nearest sideline at the free throw line extended:

    (1) Three-seconds (offensive)

    (2) Ball entering basket from below

    (3) Illegal assist in scoring

    (4) Offensive screen set out-of-bounds

    (5) Free throw violation by the offensive team

    (6) Flagrant foul-penalty (1) or (2)

    (7) Defensive three-seconds

    (8) Jump ball violation at free throw circle

    (9) Ball passing directly behind backboard

    (10) Offensive basket interference

    (11) Ball hitting horizontal basket support

    (12) Loose ball fouls which occur inside the free throw line extended

    (13) Five second back-to-the-basket violation

f. On the following infractions, the ball shall be awarded to the opposing team on the baseline at the nearest spot outside the three-second area extended:

    (1) Ball out-of-bounds on baseline

    (2) Ball hitting vertical basket support

    (3) Defensive goaltending (all privileges remain)

    (4) During a throw-in violation on the baseline

g. On the following infractions, the ball shall be awarded to the opposing team on the sideline at the nearest spot but no nearer to the baseline than the free throw line extended:

    (1) Traveling

    (2) Double dribble

    (3) Striking or kicking the ball on any situation except a throw-in

    (4) Swinging of elbows

    (5) 24-second violation

h. If the ball is kicked or punched during any throw-in, the ball will be returned to the original throw-in spot with all privileges, if any, remaining.

i. On any play where the ball goes out-of-bounds on the sideline, the ball shall be awarded to the opposing team at that spot.

j. Following a regular or 20-second timeout that was called while the ball was alive, the ball shall be awarded out-of-bounds on the sideline at the nearest spot upon resumption of play. For all other timeouts, play shall resume where it was interrupted.

    EXCEPTION: Rule 5—Section VII—e.

k. On a violation which requires putting the ball in play in the backcourt, the official will give the ball to the offensive player as soon as he is in a position out-of-bounds and ready to accept the ball.

    EXCEPTION: In the last two minutes of each period or overtime, a reasonable amount of time shall be allowed for a substitution.

## Section II—Live Ball

a. The ball becomes live when:
  (1) It is tossed by an official on any jump ball
  (2) It is at the disposal of the offensive player for a throw-in
  (3) It is placed at the disposal of a free throw shooter

## Section III—Ball is Alive

a. The ball becomes alive when:
  (1) It is legally tapped by one of the participants of a jump ball
  (2) It is released by the thrower-in
  (3) It is released by the free throw shooter on a free throw which will remain in play

## Section IV—Dead Ball

a. The ball becomes dead and/or remains dead when the following occurs:
  (1) Official blows his/her whistle
  (2) Free throw which will not remain in play (free throw which will be followed by another free throw, technical, flagrant, etc.)
  (3) Following a successful field goal or free throw that will remain in play, until player possession out-of-bounds. Contact which is NOT considered unsportsmanlike shall be ignored. (Rule 12A—Section VII—i)
  (4) Time expires for the end of any period

EXCEPTION: If a live ball is in flight, the ball becomes dead when the goal is made, missed or touched by an offensive player.

## Section V—Jump Balls in Center Circle

a. The ball shall be put into play in the center circle by a jump ball between any two opponents:
  (1) At the start of the game
  (2) At the start of each overtime period
  (3) A double free throw violation
  (4) Double foul during a loose ball situation
  (5) The ball becomes dead when neither team is in control and no field goal or infraction is involved
  (6) The ball comes to rest on the basket flange or becomes lodged between the basket ring and the backboard
  (7) A double foul which occurs as a result of a difference in opinion between officials
  (8) A suspension of play occurs during a loose ball
  (9) A fighting foul occurs during a loose ball situation

b. In all cases above, the jump ball shall be between any two opponents in the game at that time. If injury, ejection or disqualification makes it necessary for any player to be replaced, his substitute may not participate in the jump ball.

### Section VI—Other Jump Balls

a. The ball shall be put into play by a jump ball at the circle which is closest to the spot where:

    (1) A held ball occurs

    (2) A ball out-of-bounds caused by both teams

    (3) An official is in doubt as to who last touched the ball

b. The jump ball shall be between the two involved players unless injury or ejection precludes one of the jumpers from participation. If the injured or ejected player must leave the game, the coach of the opposing team shall select from his opponent's bench a player who will replace the injured or ejected player. The injured player will not be permitted to re-enter the game.

### Section VII—Restrictions Governing Jump Balls

a. Each jumper must have at least one foot on or inside that half of the jumping circle which is farthest from his own basket. Each jumper must have both feet within the restraining circle.

b. The ball must be tapped by one or both of the players participating in the jump ball after it reaches its highest point. If the ball falls to the floor without being tapped by at least one of the jumpers, the official off the ball shall whistle the ball dead and signal another toss.

c. Neither jumper may tap the tossed ball before it reaches its highest point.

d. Neither jumper may leave his half of the jumping circle until the ball has been tapped.

e. Neither jumper may catch the tossed or tapped ball until it touches one of the eight non-jumpers, the floor, the basket or the backboard.

f. Neither jumper is permitted to tap the ball more than twice on any jump ball.

g. The eight non-jumpers will remain outside the restraining circle until the ball has been tapped. Teammates may not occupy adjacent positions around the restraining circle if an opponent desires one of the positions. No player may position himself immediately behind an opponent on the restraining circle.

Penalty for c., d., e., f., g.: Ball awarded out-of-bounds to the opponent.

h. Player position on the restraining circle is determined by the direction of a player's basket. The player whose basket is nearest shall have first choice of position, with position being alternated thereafter.

## RULE NO. 7—24-SECOND CLOCK

### Section I—Definition

For the purpose of clarification the 24-second device shall be referred to as "the 24-second clock."

### Section II—Starting and Stopping of 24-Second Clock

a. The 24-second clock will start when a team gains new possession of a ball which is in play.

b. On a throw-in, the 24-second clock shall start when the ball is legally touched on the court by a player.

c. A team must attempt a field goal within 24 seconds after gaining possession of the ball. To constitute a legal field goal attempt, the following conditions must be complied with:

(1) The ball must leave the player's hand prior to the expiration of 24 seconds.

(2) After leaving the player's hand(s), the ball must make contact with the basket ring.

d. A team is considered in possession of the ball when holding, passing or dribbling. The team is considered in possession of the ball even though the ball has been batted away but the opponent has not gained possession.

e. Team possession ends when:

(1) There is a legal field goal attempt

(2) The opponent gains possession

f. If a ball is touched by a defensive player who does not gain possession of the ball, the 24-second clock shall continue to run.

g. If a defensive player causes the ball to go out-of-bounds or causes the ball to enter the basket ring from below, the 24-second clock is stopped and the offensive team shall be awarded the ball.

The offensive team shall have only the unexpired time remaining on the 24-second clock in which to attempt a field goal. If the 24-second clock reads 0, a 24-second violation has occurred, even though the horn may not have sounded.

h. If during any period there are 24 seconds OR LESS left to play in the period, the 24-second clock shall not function following a change of possession.

i. If an official inadvertently blows his whistle and the 24-second clock buzzer sounds while the ball is in the air, play shall be suspended and play resumed by a jump ball between any two opponents at the center circle, if the shot hits the rim and is unsuccessful. If the shot does not hit the rim, a 24-second violation has occurred. If the shot is successful, the goal shall count and the ball inbounded as after any successful field goal. It should be noted that even though the official blows his whistle, all provisions of the above rule apply.

j. If there is a question whether or not an attempt to score has been made within the 24 seconds allowed, the final decision shall be made by the officials.

k. Whenever the 24-second clock reads 0 and the ball is dead for any reason other than a defensive three-second violation, kicking violation, punched ball violation, personal foul or a technical foul by the defensive team, a 24-second violation has occurred.

### Section III—Putting Ball In Play After Violation

If a team fails to attempt a field goal within the time allotted, a 24-second violation shall be called. The ball is awarded to the defensive team at the sideline, nearest the spot where play was suspended but no nearer to the baseline than the free throw line extended.

### Section IV—Resetting 24-Second Clock

a. The 24-second clock shall be reset when a special situation occurs which warrants such action.

b. The 24-second clock is never reset on technical fouls and/or delay-of-game warnings called on the offensive team.

c. The 24-second clock shall be reset to 24 seconds anytime the following occurs:
   (1) Change of possession
   (2) Ball from the playing court contacting the basket ring of the team which is in possession
   (3) Personal foul where ball is being inbounded in backcourt
   (4) Violation where ball is being inbounded in backcourt
   (5) Jump balls which are not the result of a held ball caused by the defense
   (6) All flagrant and punching fouls

d. The 24-second clock shall remain the same as when play was interrupted or reset to 14 seconds, whichever is greater, anytime the following occurs:
   (1) Personal foul by the defense where ball is being inbounded in frontcourt
   (2) Defensive three-second violation
   (3) Technical fouls and/or delay-of-game warnings on the defensive team
   (4) Kicked or punched ball by the defensive team with the ball being inbounded in the offensive team's frontcourt
   (5) Infection control
   (6) Jump balls retained by the offensive team as the result of any violation by the defensive team during a jump ball which results in a frontcourt throw-in

e. The 24-second clock shall remain the same as when play was interrupted or reset to 5 seconds, whichever is greater, any time on jump balls retained by the offensive team as the result of a held ball caused by the defense

## RULE NO. 8—OUT-OF-BOUNDS AND THROW-IN
### Section I—Player
The player is out-of-bounds when he touches the floor or any object on or outside a boundary. For location of a player in the air, his position is that from which he last touched the floor.

### Section II—Ball
a. The ball is out-of-bounds when it touches a player who is out-of-bounds or any other person, the floor, or any object on, above or outside of a boundary or the supports or back of the backboard.

b. Any ball that rebounds or passes directly behind the backboard, in either direction, from any point is considered out-of-bounds.

c. The ball is caused to go out-of-bounds by the last player to touch it before it goes out, provided it is out-of-bounds because of touching something other than a player. If the ball is out-of-bounds because of touching a player who is on or outside a boundary, such player caused it to go out.

d. If the ball goes out-of-bounds and was last touched simultaneously by two opponents, both of whom are inbounds or out-of-bounds, or if the official is in doubt as to who last touched the ball, or if the officials disagree, play shall be resumed by a jump ball between the two involved players in the nearest restraining circle.

e. After the ball is out-of-bounds, the team shall designate a player to make the throw-in. He shall make the throw-in at the spot out-of-bounds nearest where the ball crossed the boundary. The designated thrower-in shall not be changed unless the offensive team makes a substitution or there is a regular or 20-second timeout.

f. If the ball is interfered with by an opponent seated on the bench or standing on the sideline (Rule 12A—Section II—a[7]), it shall be awarded to the offended team out-of-bounds nearest the spot of the violation.

## Section III—The Throw-In

a. The throw-in starts when the ball is at the disposal of a player entitled to the throw-in. He shall release the ball inbounds within 5 seconds from the time the throw-in starts. Until the passed ball has crossed the plane of the boundary, no player shall have any part of his person over the boundary line and teammates shall not occupy positions parallel or adjacent to the baseline if an opponent desires one of those positions. The defensive man shall have the right to be between his man and the basket.

b. On a throw-in which goes out of bounds and is not touched by a player in the game, the ball is returned to the original throw-in spot.

c. After a score, field goal or free throw, the latter coming as the result of a personal foul, any player of the team not credited with the score shall put the ball into play from any point out-of-bounds at the endline of the court where the point(s) were scored. He may pass the ball to a teammate behind the endline; however, the five-second throw-in rule applies.

d. After a free throw violation by the shooter or his teammate, the throw-in is made from out-of-bounds at either end of the free throw line extended.

e. Any ball out-of-bounds in a team's frontcourt or at the midcourt line cannot be passed into the backcourt. On all backcourt and midcourt violations, the ball shall be awarded to the opposing team at the midcourt line, and must be passed into the frontcourt.

EXCEPTION: During the last two minutes of the fourth period and/or any overtime period, the ball may be passed anywhere (frontcourt or backcourt) on the court.

f. A throw-in which touches the floor, or any object on or outside the boundary line, or touches anything above the playing surface is a violation. The ball must be thrown directly inbounds.

EXCEPTION: Rule 8—Section III—c.

PENALTY: Violation of this rule is loss of possession, and the ball must be inbounded at the previous spot of the throw-in.

## RULE NO. 9—FREE THROWS AND PENALTIES

### Section I—Positions and Violations

a. When a free throw is awarded, an official shall put the ball in play by placing it at the disposal of the free throw shooter. The shooter shall be above the free throw line and within the upper half of the free throw circle. He shall attempt the free throw within 10 seconds in such a way that the ball enters the basket or touches the ring.

PENALTY:

If there is a violation and the free throw attempt is to remain in play, the opposing team shall inbound on either sideline at the free throw line extended. If both teams commit a violation during this free throw, a jump ball shall be administered at midcourt between any two opponents in the game. If the opponent's violation is disconcertion, then a substitute free throw shall be awarded.

If there is a violation and the free throw attempt is not to remain in play, then play will continue from that point. If an opponent also commits a violation (double violation), then play will also continue from that point. If the opponent's violation is disconcertion, then a substitute free throw shall be awarded.

    b. The free throw shooter may not step over the plane of the free throw line until the ball touches the basket ring, backboard or the free throw ends.

PENALTY:

This is a violation by the shooter on all free throw attempts and no point can be scored.

If there is a violation and the free throw attempt is to remain in play, the opposing team shall inbound on either sideline at the free throw line extended. If both teams commit a violation during this free throw, a jump ball shall be administered at midcourt between any two opponents in the game.

If there is a violation and the free throw attempt is not to remain in play, then play will continue from that point. If an opponent also commits a violation (double violation), then play will also continue from that point.

    c. The free throw shooter shall not purposely fake a free throw attempt.

PENALTY:

This is a violation by the shooter on all free throw attempts and a double violation should not be called if an opponent violates any free throw rules.

If the free throw attempt is to remain in play, the opposing team shall inbound on either sideline at the free throw line extended.

If the free throw attempt is not to remain in play, then play will continue from that point.

    d. During a free throw attempt for a personal foul, each of the spaces nearest the end-line must be occupied by an opponent of the free throw shooter. Teammates of the free throw shooter must occupy the next adjacent spaces on each side. Only one of the third spaces may be occupied by an opponent of the free throw shooter. It is not mandatory that either of the third spaces be occupied by an opponent but may not be occupied by a teammate. If there is a discrepancy, teammates of the free throw shooter will occupy the spaces first.

Players occupying lane spaces may not be touching the lane line or floor inside the line when the ball is released by the shooter. They may not vacate their lane space more than 3' from the lane line before the ball is released.

Players not occupying lane spaces must remain behind the three point line and may not be touching the line or floor inside the line when the ball is released.

PENALTY:

If the free throw attempt is to remain in play and a teammate of the shooter violates, no point can be scored and the opposing team will inbound on either sideline at the free throw line extended. If an opponent violates, the shooter shall receive a substitute free throw if his attempt is unsuccessful but shall be ignored if the attempt is successful. If a teammate and opponent both violate, a jump ball shall be administered at midcourt between any two opponents in the game.

If the free throw attempt is not to remain in play, no violation can occur regardless of which player or players violate since no advantage is gained unless there is a disconcertion violation by an opponent to which a substitute free throw will be awarded.

e. If the ball is to become dead after the last free throw attempt, player shall not occupy positions along the free throw lanes. All players must remain behind the three point line above the free throw line extended until the ball is released.

PENALTY:

No violations can occur regardless of which player or players violate since no advantage is gained unless there is a disconcertion violation by an opponent to which a substitute free throw will be awarded.

f. During all free throw attempts, no opponent in the game shall disconcert the shooter once the ball is placed at his disposal. The following are acts of disconcertion:
- (1) raising his arms when positioned on the lane line on a free throw which will not remain in play,
- (2) waving his arms or making a sudden movement when in the visual field of the shooter during any free throw attempt,
- (3) talking to the free throw shooter or talking in a loud disruptive manner during any free throw attempt.

PENALTY:

No penalty is assessed if the free throw is successful. a substitute free throw will be administered if the attempt is unsuccessful.

g. A player shall not touch the ball or the basket ring when the ball is using the basket ring as its lower base nor touch the ball while it is in the imaginary cylinder above the ring after touching the basket ring or backboard.

PENALTY:

If the free throw attempt is to remain in play and a teammate of the shooter violates, no point can be scored and the opposing team will inbound on either sideline at the free throw line extended. If an opponent violates, one point shall be scored and play will continue as after any successful free throw with the official administering the throw-in.

If the free throw attempt is not to remain in play, no point can be scored if the violation is by a teammate and the shooter will attempt his next free throw. One point shall be scored if the violation is by an opponent and the shooter will attempt his next free throw.

h. No player shall touch the ball before it touches the basket ring or backboard.

PENALTY:

If the free throw attempt is to remain in play and a teammate of the shooter violates, no point can be scored and the opposing team will inbound on either sideline at the free throw line extended. If an opponent violates, one point shall be scored and an additional free throw shall be awarded the same shooter.

If the free throw attempt is not to remain in play, no point can be scored if the violation is by a teammate and the shooter will attempt his next free throw. One point shall be scored if the violation is by an opponent and the shooter will attempt his next free throw.

i. During all free throw attempts, if an official suspends play before the free throw attempt is released, no violations can occur.

## Section II—Shooting of Free Throw

a. The free throw(s) awarded because of a personal foul shall be attempted by the offended player.

EXCEPTIONS:

(1) If the offended player is injured or is ejected from the game and cannot attempt the awarded free throw(s), the opposing coach shall select, from his opponent's bench, the replacement player. That player will attempt the free throw(s) and the injured player will not be permitted to re-enter the game. The substitute must remain in the game until the ball is legally touched by a player on the court.

EXCEPTION: Rule 3—Section V—e

(2) If the offended player is injured and unable to attempt the awarded free throw(s) due to any unsportsmanlike act, his coach may designate any eligible member of the squad to attempt the free throw(s). The injured player will be permitted to re-enter the game.

(3) If the offended player is disqualified and unable to attempt the awarded free throw(s), his coach shall designate an eligible substitute from the bench. That substitute will attempt the free throw(s) and cannot be removed until the ball is legally touched by a player on the court.

EXCEPTION: Rule 3—Section V—e

(4) Away from play foul—Rule 12B—Section X-a(1).

b. A free throw attempt, personal or technical, shall be illegal if an official does not handle the ball and is in the free throw lane area during the actual attempt.

c. If multiple free throws are awarded, all those which remain must be attempted, if the first and/or second attempt is nullified by an offensive player's violation.

## Section III—Time Limit

Each free throw attempt shall be made within 10 seconds after the ball has been placed at the disposal of the free-thrower.

## Section IV—Next Play

After a successful free throw which is not followed by another free throw, the ball shall be put into play by a throw-in, as after any successful field goal.

EXCEPTION: After a free throw for a foul which occurs during a dead ball which immediately precedes any period, the ball shall be put into play by the team entitled to the throw-in in the period which follows. (See Rule 6—Section I—b). This includes flagrant and punching fouls.

## RULE NO. 10—VIOLATIONS AND PENALTIES

### Section I—Out-of-Bounds

a. A player shall not cause the ball to go out-of-bounds.

PENALTY: Loss of ball. The ball is awarded to the opposing team at the boundary line nearest the spot of the violation.

EXCEPTION: On a throw-in which goes out of bounds and is not touched by a player in the game, the ball is returned to the original throw-in spot.

### Section II—Dribble

a. A player shall not run with the ball without dribbling it.

b. A player in control of a dribble who steps on or outside a boundary line, even though not touching the ball while on or outside that boundary line, shall not be allowed to return inbounds and continue his dribble. He may not even be the first player to touch the ball after he has re-established a position inbounds.

c. A player may not dribble a second time after he has voluntarily ended his first dribble.

d. A player may dribble a second time if he lost control of the ball because of:
  (1) A field goal attempt at his basket, provided the ball touches the backboard or basket ring
  (2) An opponent touching the ball
  (3) A pass or fumble which has then touched another player

PENALTY: Loss of ball. Ball is awarded to the opposing team at the sideline nearest the spot of the violation but no nearer the baseline than the foul line extended.

### Section III—Thrower-in

a. A thrower-in shall not (1) carry the ball onto the court; (2) fail to release the ball within 5 seconds; (3) touch it on the court before it has touched another player; (4) leave the designated throw-in spot; (5) throw the ball so that it enters the basket before touching anyone on the court; (6) step over the boundary line while inbounding the ball; (7) cause the ball to go out-of-bounds without being touched by a player in the game; (8) leave the playing surface to gain an advantage on a throw-in; (9) hand the ball to a player on the court.

EXCEPTION: After a field goal or free throw as a result of a personal foul, the thrower-in may run the end line or pass to a teammate behind the end line.

b. Once an official recognizes the designated player to throw the ball in, there shall be no change of the thrower-in unless the offensive team makes a substitution, there is a regular or 20-second timeout or a suspension of play.

PENALTY: Loss of ball. The ball is awarded to the opposing team at the original spot of the throw-in.

### Section IV—Strike the Ball

a. A player shall not kick the ball or strike it with the fist.

b. Kicking the ball or striking it with any part of the leg is a violation when it is an intentional act. The ball accidentally striking the foot, the leg or fist is not a violation.

c. A player may not use any part of his leg to intentionally move or secure the ball.

PENALTY:
  (1) If the violation is by the offense, the ball is awarded to the opposing team at the sideline nearest the spot of the violation but no nearer to the baseline than the free throw line extended.
  (2) If the violation is by the defense while the ball is in play, the offensive team retains possession of the ball at the sideline nearest the spot of the violation but no nearer the baseline than the foul line extended.

(3) If the violation occurs during a throw-in, the opposing team retains possession at the spot of the original throw-in with all privileges, if any, remaining.

### Section V—Jump Ball

a. A player shall not violate the jump ball rule (Rule 6—Section VII).

b. During a jump ball, a personal foul committed prior to either team obtaining possession, shall be ruled a "loose ball" foul.

If the violation or foul occurs prior to the ball being legally tapped, neither the game clock or 24-second clock shall be started.

PENALTY:
(1) In (a) above, the ball is awarded to the opposing team at the sideline nearest the spot of the violation.
(2) In (a) above, if there is a violation by each team, or if the official makes a bad toss, the toss shall be repeated with the same jumpers.
(3) In (b) above, free throws may or may not be awarded, consistent with whether the penalty is in effect (Rule 12B—Section VIII).

### Section VI—Offensive Three-Second Rule

a. An offensive player shall not remain for more than three seconds in that part of his free throw lane between the endline and extended 4' (imaginary) off the court and the farther edge of the free throw line while the ball is in control of his team.

b. Allowance may be made for a player who, having been in this area for less than three seconds, is in the act of shooting at the end of the third second. Under these conditions, the 3-second count is discontinued while his continuous motion is toward the basket. If that continuous motion ceases, the previous 3-second count is continued. This is also true if it is imminent the offensive player will exit this area.

c. The 3-second count shall not begin until the ball is in control in the offensive team's frontcourt. No violation can occur if the ball is batted away by an opponent.

PENALTY: Loss of ball. The ball is awarded to the opposing team at the sideline at the free throw line extended.

### Section VII—Defensive Three-Second Rule

a. The count starts when the offensive team is in control of the ball in the frontcourt.

b. Any defensive player, who is positioned in the 16-foot lane or the area extending 4 feet past the lane endline, must be actively guarding an opponent within three seconds. Actively guarding means being within arms length of an offensive player and in a guarding position.

c. Any defensive player may play any offensive player. The defenders may double-team any player.

d. The defensive three-second count is suspended when: (1) a player is in the act of shooting, (2) there is a loss of team control, (3) the defender is actively guarding an opponent, (4) the defender completely clears the 16-foot lane or (5) it is imminent the defender will become legal.

e. If the defender is guarding the player with the ball, he may be located in the 16-foot lane. This defender is not required to be in an actively guarding/arms distance position. If another defender actively guards the player with the ball, the original defender must actively guard an opponent or exit the 16-foot lane. Once the offensive player passes the ball, the defender must actively guard an opponent or exit the 16-foot lane.

PENALTY: A technical foul shall be assessed. The offensive team retains possession at the free throw line extended. The shot clock shall remain the same as when play was interrupted or reset to 14 seconds, whichever is greater.

### Section VIII—Eight-Second Rule

A team shall not be in continuous possession of a ball which is in its backcourt for more than 8 consecutive seconds.

EXCEPTION (1): A new 8 seconds is awarded if the defense: (1) kicks or punches the ball, (2) is assessed a personal or technical foul, or (3) is issued a delay of game warning.

EXCEPTION (2): A new 8 seconds is awarded if play is suspended to administer Comments on the Rules—N—Infection Control and all jump balls.

PENALTY: Loss of ball. The ball is awarded to the opposing team at the midcourt line.

### Section IX—Ball in Backcourt

a. A player shall not be the first to touch a ball which he or a teammate caused to go from frontcourt to backcourt while his team was in control of the ball.

EXCEPTION: Rule 8—Section III—e (EXCEPTION).

b. During a jump ball, a try for a goal, or a situation in which a player taps the ball away from a congested area, as during rebounding, in an attempt to get the ball out where player control may be secured, the ball is not in control of either team. Hence, the restriction on first touching does not apply.

PENALTY: Loss of ball. The ball is awarded to the opposing team at the midcourt line.

### Section X—Swinging of Elbows

A player shall not be allowed excessive and/or vigorous swinging of the elbows in a swinging motion (no contact) when a defensive player is nearby and the offensive player has the ball.

PENALTY: Loss of ball. The ball is awarded to the opposing team at the sideline, nearest the spot of the violation but no nearer the baseline than the foul line extended. If the violation occurs on a throw-in, the game clock shall not be started.

### Section XI—Entering Basket From Below

A player shall not cause the ball to enter the basket from below.

PENALTY: Loss of ball. The ball is awarded to the opposing team at the sideline, at the free throw line extended.

### Section XII—Illegal Assist in Scoring

a. A player may not assist himself to score by using the basket ring or backboard to lift, hold or raise himself.

b. A player may not assist a teammate to gain height while attempting to score.

PENALTY: Loss of ball. The ball is awarded to the opposing team at the free throw line extended.

## Section XIII—Traveling

a. A player who receives the ball while standing still may pivot, using either foot as the pivot foot.

b. A player who receives the ball while he is progressing or upon completion of a dribble, may use a two-count rhythm in coming to a stop, passing or shooting the ball.

The first count occurs:

(1) As he receives the ball, if either foot is touching the floor at the time he receives it.

(2) As the foot touches the floor, or as both feet touch the floor simultaneously after he receives the ball, if both feet are off the floor when he receives it.

The second occurs:

(1) After the count of one when either foot touches the floor, or both feet touch the floor simultaneously.

c. A player who comes to a stop on the count of one may pivot, using either foot as the pivot foot.

d. A player who comes to a stop on the count of two, with one foot in advance of the other, may pivot using only the rear foot as the pivot foot.

e. A player who comes to a stop on the count of two, with neither foot in advance of the other, may use either foot as the pivot foot.

f. In starting a dribble after (1) receiving the ball while standing still, or (2) coming to a legal stop, the ball must be out of the player's hand before the pivot foot is raised off the floor.

g. If a player, with the ball in his possession, raises his pivot foot off the floor, he must pass or shoot before his pivot foot returns to the floor. If he drops the ball while in the air, he may not be the first to touch the ball.

h. A player who falls to the floor while holding the ball, or while coming to a stop, may not gain an advantage by sliding.

i. A player who attempts a field goal may not be the first to touch the ball if it fails to touch the backboard, basket ring or another player.

j. A player may not be the first to touch his own pass.

PENALTY: Loss of ball. The ball is awarded to the opposing team at the sideline, nearest spot of the violation but no nearer the baseline than the foul line extended.

## Section XIV—Offensive Screen Set Out-of-Bounds

An offensive player shall not leave the playing area of the floor on the endline in the frontcourt for the purpose of setting a screen.

PENALTY: Loss of ball. The ball is awarded to the opposing team at the sideline at the free throw line extended.

## Section XV—Five-Second Back-to-the-Basket Violation

An offensive player in his frontcourt below the free throw line extended shall not be permitted to dribble with his back or side to the basket for more than five seconds.

The count ends when (1) the player picks up the ball, (2) dribbles above the free throw line extended or (3) a defensive player deflects the ball away.

PENALTY: Loss of ball. The ball is awarded to the opposing team out-of-bounds on the nearest sideline at the free throw line extended.

# RULE NO. 11—BASKETBALL INTERFERENCE—GOALTENDING

## Section I—A Player Shall Not:

a. Touch the ball or the basket ring when the ball is using the basket ring as its lower base.

EXCEPTION: If a player near his own basket has his hand legally in contact with the ball, it is not a violation if his contact with the ball continues after the ball enters the cylinder, or if, in such action, he touches the basket.

b. Touch the ball when it is above the basket ring and within the imaginary cylinder.

c. During a field goal attempt, touch a ball after it has touched any part of the backboard above ring level, whether the ball is considered on its upward or downward flight.

d. During a field goal attempt, touch a ball after it has touched the backboard below the ring level and while the ball is on its upward flight.

e. Trap the ball against the face of the backboard after it has been released. (To be a trapped ball, three elements must exist simultaneously. The hand, the ball and the backboard must all occur at the same time. A batted ball against the backboard is not a trapped ball.)

f. Touch any live ball from within the playing area that is on its downward flight with an opportunity to score. This is considered to be a "field goal attempt" or trying for a goal.

g. Touch the ball at any time with a hand which is through the basket ring.

h. Vibrate the rim, net or backboard so as to cause the ball to make an unnatural bounce.

i. Touch the ball while in the net preventing it from clearing the basket.

PENALTY: If the violation is at the opponent's basket, the offended team is awarded two points, if the attempt is from the two point zone and three points if it is from the three point zone. The crediting of the score and subsequent procedure is the same as if the awarded score has resulted from the ball having gone through the basket, except that the official shall hand the ball to a player of the team entitled to the throw-in. If the violation is at a team's own basket, no points can be scored and the ball is awarded to the offended team at the free throw line extended on either sideline. If there is a violation by both teams, play shall be resumed by a jump ball between any two opponents at the center circle.

# RULE NO. 12—FOULS AND PENALTIES

## A. Technical Foul

### Section I—Excessive Timeouts

a. Requests for a timeout in excess of the authorized number shall be granted and a technical foul shall be assessed. Following the timeout and free throw attempt, the ball will be awarded to the team which shot the free throw and play shall resume with a throw-in nearest the spot where play was interrupted.

b. If the excessive timeout is granted prior to free throw attempt(s), there will be no lineup for the remaining free throws and play shall resume with a throw-in at the point of interruption by the team which shot the technical foul.

c. If the excessive timeout is granted prior to a jump ball, the ball shall be awarded to the team shooting the technical foul at the point of interruption.

## Section II—Delay-of-Game

a. A delay-of-game shall be called for:
  (1) Preventing the ball from being promptly put into play.
  (2) Interfering with the ball after a successful field goal or free throw.
  (3) Failing to immediately pass the ball to the nearest official when a personal foul or violation is assessed.
  (4) Touching the ball before the throw-in has been released.
  (5) A defender crossing the boundary line prior to the ball being released on a throw-in.
  (6) A team preventing play from commencing at any time.
  (7) Any player, coach or trainer interfering with a ball which has crossed the boundary line (Rule 8—Section II—f).

PENALTY: The first offense is a warning. A technical foul shall be assessed with each successive offense and charged to the team. An announcement will be made by the public address announcer. The 24-second clock shall remain the same or reset to 14, whichever is greater, if the violation is assessed against the defensive team. The offensive team shall be awarded a new 8 seconds to advance the ball if it is in the backcourt. If repeated acts become a travesty, the head coach shall be notified that he is being held responsible.

EXCEPTION (5): In the last two minutes of the fourth period and/or any overtime period, a technical foul will be assessed if the defender crosses or breaks the plane of the boundary line when an offensive player is in a position to inbound and prior to the ball being released on a throw-in.

## Section III—Substitutions

a. A substitute shall report to the official scorer while standing in the "substitution box."

b. A substitute shall not enter onto the court until he is beckoned by an official.

c. A substitute shall not be allowed to re-enter the game after being disqualified.

EXCEPTION: Rule 3—Section I—b.

d. It is the responsibility of each team to have the proper number of players on the court at all times. Failure to do so will result in a technical foul being assessed and charged to the team.

EXCEPTION: If the violation occurs on (1) a free throw attempt which is to be followed by another free throw attempt, or (2) a free throw attempt that is not going to remain in play.

## Section IV—Basket Ring, Backboard or Support

a. An offensive player who deliberately hangs on his basket ring, net, backboard or support during the game shall be assessed a non-unsportsmanlike technical foul and a $500 fine.

b. A defensive player who deliberately gains or maintains height or hangs on his opponent's basket ring, net, backboard or support shall be assessed a non-unsportsmanlike technical foul. If he touches the ball during a field goal attempt, points shall be awarded consistent with the type of shot.

EXCEPTION: An offensive or defensive player may hang on the basket ring, backboard or support to prevent an injury to himself or another player, with no technical foul assessed.

c. Should a defensive player deliberately hang on the basket ring, backboard or support to successfully touch a ball which is in possession of an opponent, a non-unsportsmanlike technical foul shall be assessed.

## Section V—Conduct

a. An official may assess a technical foul, without prior warning, at any time. A technical foul(s) may be assessed to any player on the court or anyone seated on the bench for conduct which, in the opinion of an official, is detrimental to the game. A technical foul cannot be assessed for physical contact when the ball is alive.

EXCEPTION: Fighting fouls and/or taunting with physical contact.

b. A maximum of two technicals for unsportsmanlike acts may be assessed any player, coach or trainer. Any of these offenders may be ejected for committing only one unsportsmanlike act, and they must be ejected for committing two unsportsmanlike acts.

c. A technical foul called for (1) delay of game, (2) coaches box violations, (3) defensive 3-seconds, (4) having a team total of less or more than five players when the ball is alive, or (5) a player hanging on the basket ring or backboard is not considered an act of unsportsmanlike conduct.

d. A technical foul shall be assessed for unsportsmanlike tactics such as:

    (1) Disrespectfully addressing an official

    (2) Physically contacting an official

    (3) Overt actions indicating resentment to a call

    (4) Use of profanity

    (5) A coach entering onto the court without permission of an official

    (6) A deliberately-thrown elbow or any attempted physical act with no contact involved

    (7) Taunting

e. Cursing or blaspheming an official shall not be considered the only cause for imposing technical fouls. Running tirades, continuous criticism or griping may be sufficient cause to assess a technical. Excessive misconduct shall result in ejection from the game.

f. Assessment of a technical foul shall be avoided whenever and wherever possible; but, when necessary they are to be assessed without delay or procrastination. Once a player has been ejected or the game is over, technicals cannot be assessed regardless of the provocation. Any additional unsportsmanlike conduct shall be reported by E-mail immediately to the Basketball Operations Department.

g. If a technical foul is assessed to a team following a personal foul on the same team, the free throw attempt for the technical foul shall be administered first.

h. The ball shall be awarded to the team which had possession at the time the technical foul was assessed, whether the free throw attempt is successful or not. Play shall be resumed by a throw-in nearest the spot where play was interrupted.

EXCEPTION: Rule 12A—Section I.

i. Anyone guilty of illegal contact which occurs during a dead ball may be assessed (1) a technical foul, if the contact is deemed to be unsportsmanlike in nature, or (2) a flagrant foul, if unnecessary and/or excessive contact occurs.

j. Free throws awarded for a technical foul must be attempted by a player in the game when the technical foul is assessed.

> (1) If a substitute has been beckoned into the game or has been recognized by the officials as being in the game prior to a technical foul being assessed, he is eligible to attempt the free throw(s).
>
> (2) If the technical foul is assessed before the opening tap, any player listed in the scorebook as a starter is eligible to attempt the free throw(s).
>
> (3) If a technical foul is assessed before the starting lineup is indicated, any player on the squad may attempt the free throw(s).

k. A technical foul, unsportsmanlike act or flagrant foul must be called for a participant to be ejected. A player, coach or trainer may be ejected for:

(1) An elbow foul which makes contact shoulder level or below

(2) Any unsportsmanlike conduct where a technical foul is assessed

(3) A flagrant foul where unnecessary and/or excessive contact occurs

EXCEPTION: Rule 12A—Section V—l(5)

l. A player, coach or trainer must be ejected for:

(1) A punching foul

(2) A fighting foul

(3) An elbow foul which makes contact above shoulder level

(4) An attempted punch which does not make contact

(5) Deliberately entering the stands other than as a continuance of play

m. Eye guarding (placing a hand in front of the opponent's eyes when guarding from the rear) a player who does not have possession of the ball is illegal and an unsportsmanlike technical shall be assessed.

n. A free throw attempt is awarded when one technical foul is assessed.

o. No free throw attempts are awarded when a double technical foul is assessed. Technical fouls assessed to opposing teams during the same dead ball and prior to the administering of any free throw attempt for the first technical foul, shall be interpreted as a double technical foul.

p. The deliberate act of throwing the ball or any object at an official by a player, coach or trainer is a technical foul and violators are subject to ejection from the game.

q. Elbow fouls, which make contact above shoulder level, and punching fouls, although recorded as both personal and team fouls, are unsportsmanlike acts. The player will be ejected immediately.

## Section VI—Fighting Fouls

a. Technical fouls shall be assessed players, coaches or trainers for fighting. No free throws will be attempted. The participants will be ejected immediately.

b. This rule applies whether play is in progress or the ball is dead.

c. If a fighting foul occurs with a team in possession of the ball, that team will retain possession on the sideline nearest the spot where play was interrupted but no nearer to the baseline than the free throw line extended.

d. If a fighting foul occurs with neither team in possession, play will be resumed with a jump ball between any two opponents who were in the game at the center circle.

e. A fine not exceeding $35,000 and/or suspension may be imposed upon such person(s) by the Commissioner at his sole discretion.

## Section VII—Fines

a. Recipients of technical fouls for unsportsmanlike conduct will be assessed a $500 fine for the first offense, and an additional $500 for the second offense in any one given game, for a minimum total of $1,000. If a player is ejected on (1) the first technical foul for unsportsmanlike conduct, (2) a punching foul, (3) a fighting foul, (4) an elbow foul, or (5) a flagrant foul, he shall be fined a minimum of $1,000.

b. Whether or not said player(s) is ejected, a fine not exceeding $35,000 and/or suspension may be imposed upon such player(s) by the Commissioner at his sole discretion.

c. During an altercation, all players not participating in the game must remain in the immediate vicinity of their bench. Violators will be suspended, without pay, for a minimum of one game and fined up to $35,000.

The suspensions will commence prior to the start of their next game.

A team must have a minimum of eight players dressed and ready to play in every game.

If five or more players leave the bench, the players will serve their suspensions alphabetically, according to the first letters of their last name.

If seven bench players are suspended (assuming no participants are included), four of them would be suspended for the first game following the altercation. The remaining three would be suspended for the second game following the altercation.

d. A player, coach or assistant coach, upon being notified by an official that he has been ejected from the game, must leave the playing area IMMEDIATELY and remain in the dressing room of his team during such suspension until completion of the game or leave the building. Violation of this rule shall call for an automatic fine of $500. A fine not to exceed $35,000 and possible forfeiture of the game may be imposed for any violation of this rule.

e. Any player who in the opinion of the officials has deliberately hung on the basket ring shall be assessed a non-unsportsmanlike technical foul and a fine of $500.

EXCEPTION: An offensive or defensive player may hang on the basket ring, backboard or support to prevent an injury to himself or another player, with no penalty.

f. At halftime and the end of each game, the coach and his players are to leave the court and go directly to their dressing room, without pause or delay. There is to be absolutely no talking to game officials.

PENALTY—$500 fine to be doubled for any additional violation.

g. A $500 fine shall be assessed to any player(s) hanging on the rim during pre-game warm-up. Officials shall be present during warm-up to observe violations.

h. Any player who is assessed a flagrant foul—penalty (2) must be ejected and will be fined a minimum of $1,000. The incident will be reported to the Basketball Operations Department.

## B. Personal Foul

### Section I—Types

a. A player shall not hold, push, charge into, impede the progress of an opponent by extending a hand, forearm, leg or knee or by bending the body into a position that is not normal. Contact that results in the re-routing of an opponent is a foul which must be called immediately.

b. Contact initiated by the defensive player guarding a player with the ball is not legal. This contact includes, but is not limited to, forearm, hands, or body check.

EXCEPTIONS:
- (1) A defender may apply contact with a forearm to an offensive player with the ball who has his back to the basket below the free throw line extended outside the Lower Defensive Box.
- (2) A defender may apply contact with a forearm and/or one hand with a bent elbow to an offensive player in a post-up position with the ball in the Lower Defensive Box.
- (3) A defender may apply contact with a forearm to an offensive player with the ball at any time in the Lower Defensive Box.

The forearm in the above exceptions is solely for the purpose of maintaining a defensive position.

- (4) A defender may position his leg between the legs of an offensive player in a post-up position in the Lower Defensive Box for the purpose of maintaining defensive position. If his foot leaves the floor in an attempt to dislodge his opponent, it is a foul immediately.
- (5) Incidental contact with the hand against an offensive player shall be ignored if it does not affect the player's speed, quickness, balance and/or rhythm.

c. Any player whose actions against an opponent cause illegal contact with yet another opponent has committed the personal foul.

d. A personal foul committed by the offensive team during a throw-in shall be an offensive foul, regardless of whether the ball has been released.

e. Contact which occurs on the hand of the offensive player, while that hand is in contact with the ball, is legal.

EXCEPTION: Flagrant, elbow and punching fouls.

PENALTIES: The offender is charged with a personal foul. The offended team is charged with a team foul if the illegal contact was caused by the defender. There is no team foul if there are personal fouls on one member of each team or the personal foul is against an offensive player. The offended team is awarded:

(1) the ball out-of-bounds on the sideline at the nearest spot where play was interrupted but no nearer to the baseline than the free throw line extended if an offensive foul is assessed.

(2) the ball out-of-bounds on the sideline where play was interrupted but no nearer to the baseline than the free throw line extended if the personal foul is on the defender and if the penalty situation is not in effect.

(3) one free throw attempt if the personal foul is on the defender and there is a successful field goal or free throw on the play.

(4) two/three free throw attempts if the personal foul is on the defender and the offensive player is in the act of shooting an unsuccessful field goal.

(5) one free throw attempt plus a penalty free throw attempt if the personal foul is on the defender and the offensive player is not in the act of attempting a field goal if the penalty situation is in effect.

(6) one free throw attempt and possession of the ball on the sideline nearest the spot where play was interrupted if an offensive player, or a teammate, is fouled while having a clear-path-to-the-basket. The ball and an offensive player must be positioned between the tip-of-circle extended in the backcourt and the basket in the frontcourt, with no defender between the ball and the basket when the personal foul occurs. There must be team control and the new play must originate in the backcourt, including throw-ins, and the offended team must be deprived of an opportunity to score an uncontested basket.

(7) two free throw attempts if the personal foul is for illegal contact with an elbow. The elbow foul may be assessed whether the ball is dead or alive. Free throw attempts are awarded whether the ball is dead, alive, loose or away-from-the-play in the last two minutes of regulation or overtime(s).

Contact must occur for an elbow foul to be assessed. It is an unsportsmanlike act whether or not there is contact. (See Rule 12A—Section V—d(6) for non-contact.)

If the deliberate elbow contact is above shoulder level, the player will be ejected. If the elbow contact is shoulder level or below, the player may be ejected at the discretion of the official.

In all of these situations, the official has the discretion of assessing a flagrant foul (1) or (2).

(8) two free throw attempts if a personal foul is committed by a defender prior to the ball being released on a throw-in.

EXCEPTION: Rule 12B—Section X.

(9) two free throw attempts if a personal foul is committed against an offensive player without the ball when his team has at least a one-man advantage on a fast break and the defensive player takes a foul to stop play.

## Section II—By Dribbler

a. A dribbler shall not (1) charge into an opponent who has established a legal guarding position, or (2) attempt to dribble between two opponents, or (3) attempt to dribble between an opponent and a boundary, where sufficient space is not available for illegal contact to be avoided.

b. If a defender is able to establish a legal position in the straight line path of the dribbler, the dribbler must avoid contact by changing direction or ending his dribble.

c. The dribbler must be in control of his body at all times. If illegal contact occurs, the responsibility is on the dribbler.

PENALTY: The offender is assessed an offensive foul. There is no team foul. The ball is awarded to the offended team on the sideline nearest the spot where play was interrupted but no nearer to the baseline than the free throw line extended.

EXCEPTION: Rule 3—Section I—a.

d. If a dribbler has sufficient space to have his head and shoulders in advance of his defender, the responsibility for illegal contact is on the defender.

e. If a dribbler has established a straight line path, a defender may not crowd him out of that path.

PENALTY: The defender shall be assessed a personal foul and a team foul. If the penalty is not in effect, the offended team is awarded the ball on the sideline nearest the spot where play was interrupted but no nearer to the baseline than the free throw line extended. If the penalty is in effect, one free throw attempt plus a penalty free throw attempt is awarded.

### Section III—By Screening

A player who sets a screen shall not (1) assume a position nearer than a normal step from an opponent, if that opponent is stationary and unaware of the screener's position, or (2) make illegal contact with an opponent when he assumes a position at the side or front of an opponent, or (3) assume a position so near to a moving opponent that illegal contact cannot be avoided by the opponent without changing direction or stopping, or (4) move laterally or toward an opponent being screened, after having assumed a legal position. The screener may move in the same direction and path of the opponent being screened.

In (3) above, the speed of the opponent being screened will determine what the screener's stationary position may be. This position will vary and may be one to two normal steps or strides from his opponent.

### Section IV—Flagrant Foul

a. If contact committed against a player, with or without the ball, is interpreted to be unnecessary, a flagrant foul—penalty (1) will be assessed. A personal foul is charged to the offender and a team foul is charged to the team.

PENALTY: (1) Two free throws shall be attempted and the ball awarded to the offended team on either side of the court at the free throw line extended. (2) If the offended player is injured and unable to attempt his free throws, the opposing coach will select any player from the bench to attempt the free throws. (3) This substitute may not be replaced until the ball is legally touched by a player on the court. (EXCEPTION: Rule 3—Section V—e.) (4) The injured player may not return to the game. (5) A player will be ejected if he commits two flagrant fouls in the same game.

b. If contact committed against a player, with or without the ball, is interpreted to be unnecessary and excessive, a flagrant foul—penalty (2) will be assessed. A personal foul is charged to the offender and a team foul is charged to the team.

PENALTY: (1) Two free throws shall be attempted and the ball awarded to the offended team on either side of the court at the free throw line extended. (2) If the offended player is injured and unable to attempt his free throws, his coach will select a substitute and any player from the team is eligible to attempt the free throws. (3) This substitute may not be replaced until the ball is legally touched by a player on the court. EXCEPTION: Rule 3—Section V—e. (4) The injured player may return to the game at any time after the free throws are attempted. (5) This is an unsportsmanlike act and the offender is ejected.

c. A flagrant foul may be assessed whether the ball is dead or alive.

## Section V—Free Throw Penalty Situations

a. Each team is limited to four team fouls per regulation period without additional penalties. Common fouls charged as team fouls, in excess of four, will be penalized by one free throw attempt plus a penalty free throw attempt.

    (1) The first four common fouls committed by a team in any regulation period shall result in the ball being awarded to the opposing team on the sideline nearest where play was interrupted. The ball shall be awarded no nearer to the baseline than the free throw line extended.

    (2) The first three common fouls committed by a team in any overtime period, shall result in the ball being awarded to the opposing team on the sideline nearest where play was interrupted. The ball shall be awarded no nearer to the baseline than the free throw line extended.

    (3) If a team has not committed its quota of four team fouls during the first ten minutes of any regulation period, or its quota of three team fouls during the first three minutes of any overtime period, it shall be permitted to incur one team foul during the last two minutes without penalty.

    (4) During any overtime period, common fouls charged as team fouls in excess of three, will be penalized by one free throw plus a penalty free throw attempt.

    (5) Personal fouls which are flagrant, punching, elbowing, away-from-the-play, or clear-path-to-the-basket will carry their own separate penalties and are included in the team foul total.

    (6) Personal fouls committed during a successful field goal attempt, which result in one free throw attempt being awarded, will not result in an additional free throw attempt if the penalty situation exists.

b. A maximum of three points may be scored by the same team on a successful two-point field goal attempt.

c. A maximum of four points may be scored by the same team on a successful three-point field goal attempt.

## Section VI—Double Fouls

a. No free throw attempts will be awarded on double fouls, whether they are personal or technical.

b. Double personal fouls shall add to a player's total, but not to the team total.

c. If a double foul occurs, the team in possession of the ball at the time of the call shall retain possession. Play is resumed on the sideline, nearest the point where play was interrupted but no nearer to the baseline than the free throw line extended. The 24-second clock is reset to 24 seconds if the ball is to be inbounded in the team's backcourt or stay the same or reset to 14, whichever is greater, if the ball is to be inbounded in the frontcourt.

d. If a double foul occurs with neither team in possession, or when the ball is in the air on an unsuccessful field goal or free throw attempt, play will be resumed with a jump ball at the center circle between any two opponents in the game at that time. If injury, ejection or disqualification makes it necessary for any player to be replaced, no substitute may participate in the jump ball. The jumper shall be selected from one of the remaining players in the game.

e. If a double foul occurs on a successful field goal or free throw attempt, the team that has been scored upon will inbound the ball at the baseline as after any other score.

f. If a double foul occurs as a result of a difference in opinion by the officials, no points can be scored and play shall resume with a jump ball at the center circle between any two opponents in the game at that time. No substitute may participate in the jump ball.

### Section VII—Offensive Fouls

A personal foul assessed against an offensive player which is neither an elbow, punching or flagrant foul shall be penalized in the following manner:

    (1) No points can be scored by the offensive team

    (2) The offending player is charged with a personal foul

    (3) The offending team is not charged with a team foul

EXCEPTION: Rule 3—Section I—a. No penalty free throws are awarded.

    (4) The ball is awarded to the offended team out-of-bounds on the sideline at the nearest spot where play was interrupted but no nearer the baseline than the free throw line extended

### Section VIII—Loose Ball Fouls

a. A personal foul, which is neither a punching, flagrant or an elbow foul, committed while there is no team control shall be administered in the following manner:

    (1) Offending team is charged with a team foul

    (2) Offending player is charged with a personal foul

    (3) Offended team will be awarded possession at the sideline, nearest the spot where play was interrupted but no nearer the baseline than the foul line extended, if no penalty exists

    (4) Offended player is awarded one free throw attempt plus a penalty free throw attempt if the offending team is in a penalty situation

b. If a "loose ball" foul called against the defensive team is then followed by a successful field goal, one free throw attempt will be awarded to the offended player, allowing for the three point or four point play. This interpretation applies:

    (1) Regardless of which offensive player is fouled

    (2) Whether or not the penalty situation exists. The ball can never be awarded to the scoring team out-of-bounds following a personal foul which occurs on the same play

c. If a "loose ball" foul called against the defensive team is followed by a successful free throw, one free throw will be awarded to the offended player whether or not the penalty is in effect.

d. If a "loose ball" foul called against the offensive team is then followed by a successful field goal attempt by the same offensive player, no points may be scored.

### Section IX—Punching Fouls

a. Illegal contact called on a player for punching is a personal foul and a team foul. One free throw attempt shall be awarded, regardless of the number of previous fouls in the period. The ball shall be awarded to the offended team out-of-bounds on either side of the court at the free throw line extended whether the free throw is successful or unsuccessful.

b. Any player who throws a punch, whether it connects or not, has committed an unsportsmanlike act. He will be ejected immediately and suspended for a minimum of one game.

c. This rule applies whether play is in progress or the ball is dead.

d. In the case where one punching foul is followed by another, all aspects of the rule are applied in both cases, and the team last offended is awarded possession on the sideline at the free throw line extended in the frontcourt.

e. A fine not exceeding $35,000 and/or suspension may be imposed upon such player(s) by the Commissioner at his sole discretion.

### Section X—Away-From-The-Play Foul

a. During the last two minutes of the fourth period or overtime period(s) with the offensive team in possession of the ball, all personal fouls which are assessed against the defensive team prior to the ball being released on a throw-in and/or away-from-the-play, shall be administered as follows:

- (1) A personal foul and team foul shall be assessed and one free throw attempt shall be awarded. The free throw may be attempted by any player in the game at the time the personal foul was committed.
- (2) If the foul occurs when the ball is inbounds, the offended team shall be awarded the ball at the nearest point where play was interrupted but no nearer to the baseline than the free throw line extended.
- (3) If the foul occurs prior to the release on a throw-in, the offended team shall be awarded the ball at the original throw-in spot, with all privileges, if any, remaining.

EXCEPTION: Rule 12-B—Section X-b and c.

b. In the event that the personal foul committed is an elbow foul, the play shall be administered as follows:

- (1) A personal foul and team foul shall be assessed and the free throw shooter shall be awarded two free throw attempts. The free throw(s) may be attempted by any player in the game at the time the personal foul was committed.
- (2) In the event that the offended player is unable to participate in the game, the free throw shooter may be selected by his coach from any eligible player on the team. Any substitute must remain in the game until the ball is legally touched by a player on the court.

    EXCEPTION: Rule 3—Section V—e.

- (3) The offended team shall be awarded the ball at the nearest point where play was interrupted with all privileges remaining.

c. In the event that the personal foul committed is a flagrant foul, the play shall be administered as follows:

- (1) A personal foul and team foul shall be assessed and the free throw shooter shall be awarded two free throw attempts. The free throws may be attempted by any player in the game at the time the flagrant foul was committed.
- (2) If a flagrant foul—penalty (1) is assessed and the offended player is unable to participate in the game, the substitute will be selected by his coach. The two free throws may be attempted by any of the four remain-

ing players in the game. The ball will be awarded to the offended team at the free throw line extended in the frontcourt. The injured player may return to the game.

(3) If a flagrant foul—penalty (2) is assessed and the offended player is unable to participate in the game, the substitute will be selected by his coach. The two free throws may be attempted by the substitute or any of the four remaining players in the game. The ball will be awarded to the offended team at the free throw line extended in the frontcourt. The injured player may return to the game.

## RULE NO. 13—INSTANT REPLAY

### Section I—Instant Replay Review Triggers

a. Instant replay would be triggered automatically in the following situations:

(1) A field goal made with no time remaining on the clock (0:00) at the end of the fourth period or any overtime period that, if scored, would affect or potentially could affect, the outcome of the game.

(2) A field goal made with no time remaining on the clock (0:00) at the end of the first, second and third periods.

(3) A foul called with no time remaining on the clock (0:00) at the end of the fourth period or any overtime period, provided that the resulting free throws could affect the outcome of the game.

(4) A foul called with no time remaining on the clock (0:00) at the end of the first, second or third periods.

### Section II—Reviewable Matters

a. If an instant replay review is triggered as described in Section I—a (1) and (2) above, the officials would review the tape to determine only the following issues:

(1) Whether time on the game clock expired before the ball left the shooter's hand.

(2) If the shot was timely, whether the successful field goal was scored correctly as a two-point or three-point field goal.

(3) If the shot was timely, whether the shooter committed a boundary line violation. For purposes of this review, the official would look only at the position of the shooter's feet at the moment they last touched the floor immediately prior to (or, if applicable, during) the release of the shot.

(4) Whether the 24-second clock expired before the ball left the shooter's hand.

(5) Whether an 8-second backcourt violation occurred before the ball left the shooter's hand.

(6) Whether a called foul that is **not** committed on or by a player in the act of shooting occurred prior to the expiration on the game clock. For a called foul that **is** committed on or by a player in the act of shooting, where the shooter releases the ball prior to expiration of time on the game clock, the foul should be administered regardless of whether it occurred prior to or after the expiration of time.

b. If an instant replay review is triggered as described in Section I—a (3) and (4) above, the officials would review the tape to determine only the following issue:

(1) Whether the called foul occurred prior to the expiration of time on the game clock.

NOTE: The officials would be permitted to utilize instant replay to determine whether (and how much) time should be put on the game clock but only when it is determined through replay that (i) the shooter committed a boundary line violation, (ii) a 24-second violation occurred, (iii) an 8-second backcourt violation occurred, or (iv) a called foul occurred prior to the expiration of time on the game clock.

### Section III—Replay Review Process

a. All replay reviews would be conducted by the officials as a crew after gathering as much information as possible. In cases of conflict, the crew chief would make the final decision.

b. The call made by the game officials during play would be reversed only when the replay provides the officials with "clear and conclusive" visual evidence to do so.

## COMMENTS ON THE RULES
## I. GUIDES FOR ADMINISTRATION AND APPLICATION OF THE RULES

Each official should have a definite and clear conception of his/her overall responsibilities. It is essential for them to know, understand and implement the rules as intended. If all officials possess the same conception there will be a guaranteed uniformity in the administration of all contests.

The restrictions placed upon the player by the rules are intended to create a balance of play, equal opportunity for the defense and the offense, provide reasonable safety and protection for all players and emphasize cleverness and skill without unduly limiting freedom of action of player or team.

The purpose of penalties is to compensate a player who has been placed at a disadvantage through an illegal act of an opponent and to restrain players from committing acts which, if ignored, might lead to roughness even though they do not affect the immediate play. To implement this philosophy, there are times during a game where "degrees of certainty" are necessary to determine a foul during physical contact. This practice may be necessary throughout the game with a higher degree implemented during impact times when the intensity is risen, especially nearing the end of a game.

## II. BASIC PRINCIPLES
### A. CONTACT SITUATIONS
#### 1. Incidental Contact

The mere fact that contact occurs does not necessarily constitute a foul. Contact which is incidental to an effort by a player to play an opponent, reach a loose ball, or perform normal defensive or offensive movements, should not be considered illegal. If, however, a player attempts to play an opponent from a position where he has no reasonable chance to perform without making contact with his opponent, the responsibility is on the player in this position.

The hand is considered "part of the ball" when it is in contact with the ball. Therefore, contact on that hand by a defender while it is in contact with the ball is not illegal.

#### 2. Guarding an Opponent

In all guarding situations, a player is entitled to any spot on the court he desires, provided he legally gets to that spot first and without contact with an opponent. If a defensive or offensive player has established a position on the floor and his opponent initiates contact that results in the dislodging of the opponent, a foul should be called IMMEDIATELY.

During all throw-ins, the defensive player(s) must be allowed to take a position between his man and the basket.

A player may continue to move after gaining a guarding position in the path of an opponent provided he is not moving directly or obliquely toward his opponent when contact occurs. A player is never permitted to move into the path of an opponent after the opponent has jumped into the air.

A player who extends a hand, forearm, shoulder, hip or leg into the path of an opponent and thereby causes contact is not considered to have a legal position in the path of an opponent.

A player is entitled to a vertical position even to the extent of holding his arms above his shoulders, as in post play or when double-teaming in pressing tactics.

Any player who conforms to the above is absolved from responsibility for any contact by an opponent which may dislodge or tend to dislodge such player from the position which he has attained and is maintaining legally. If contact occurs, the official must decide whether the contact is incidental or a foul has been committed.

### 3. Screening

When a player screens in front of or at the side of a stationary opponent, he may be as close as he desires providing he does not make contact. His opponent can see him and, therefore, is expected to detour around the screen.

If he screens behind a stationary opponent, the opponent must be able to take a normal step backward without contact. Because the opponent is not expected to see a screener behind him, the player screened is given latitude of movement. The defender must be given an opportunity to change direction and avoid contact with the screener.

To screen a moving opponent, the player must stop soon enough to permit his opponent to stop or change direction. The distance between the player screening and his opponent will depend upon the speed at which the players are moving.

If two opponents are moving in the same direction and path, the player who is behind is responsible for contact. The player in front may stop or slow his pace, but he may not move backward or sidewards into his opponent. The player in front may or may not have the ball. This situation assumes the two players have been moving in identically the same direction and path before contact.

### 4. The Dribble

If the dribbler's path is blocked, he is expected to pass or shoot; that is, he should not try to dribble by an opponent unless there is a reasonable chance of getting by without contact.

## B. FOULS: FLAGRANT—UNSPORTSMANLIKE

To be unsportsmanlike is to act in a manner unbecoming to the image of professional basketball. It consists of acts of deceit, disrespect of officials and profanity. The penalty for such action is a technical foul. Repeated acts shall result in expulsion from the game and a minimum fine of $1000.

A flagrant foul—penalty (1) is unnecessary contact committed by a player against an opponent.

A flagrant foul—penalty (2) is unnecessary and excessive contact committed by a player against an opponent. It is an unsportsmanlike act and the offender is ejected immediately.

The offender will be subject to a fine not exceeding $35,000 and/or suspension by the Commissioner.

See Rule 12B—Section IV for interpretation and penalties.

## C. BLOCK-CHARGE

A defensive player is permitted to establish a legal guarding position in the path of a dribbler regardless of his speed and distance.

A defensive player is not permitted to move into the path of an offensive player once he has started his shooting motion.

A defensive player must allow a moving player the distance to stop or change direction when the offensive player receives a pass outside the lower defensive box. The lower defensive box is the area between the 3-foot posted-up marks, the bottom tip of the circle and the endline.

A defensive player must allow an alighted player the distance to land and then stop or change direction when the offensive player is outside the lower defensive box.

A defensive player is permitted to establish a legal guarding position in the path of an offensive player who receives a pass inside the lower defensive box regardless of his speed and distance.

A defensive player must allow an alighted player who receives a pass the space to land when the offensive player is inside the lower defensive box.

A player must allow a moving opponent without the ball the distance to stop or change direction.

The speed of the player will determine the amount of distance an opponent must allow.

If an offensive player causes contact with a defensive player who has established a legal position, an offensive foul shall be called and no points may be scored. A defensive player may turn slightly to protect himself, but is never allowed to bend over and submarine an opponent.

An offensive foul should not be called for charging if the contact is with a secondary defensive player who has established a defensive position within a designated "restricted area" near the basket for the purpose of drawing an offensive foul. The "restricted area" for this purpose is the area bounded by an arc with a 4-foot radius measured from the middle of the basket.

EXCEPTION: Any player may be legally positioned within the "restricted area" if the offensive player receives the ball within the Lower Defensive Box.

The mere fact that contact occurs on these type of plays, or any other similar play, does not necessarily mean that a personal foul has been committed. The officials must decide whether the contact is negligible and/or incidental, judging each situation separately.

## D. GAME CANCELLATION

For the purpose of game cancellation, the officials' jurisdiction begins with the opening tipoff. Prior to this, it shall be the decision of the home management whether or not playing conditions are such to warrant postponement.

However, once the game begins, if because of extremely hazardous playing conditions the question arises whether or not the game should be cancelled, the crew chief shall see that EVERY effort is made to continue the game before making the decision to terminate it.

## E. PHYSICAL CONTACT—SUSPENSION

Any player or coach guilty of intentional physical contact with an official shall automatically be suspended without pay for one game. A fine and/or longer period of suspension will result if circumstances so dictate.

## F. PROTEST

Protests are not permitted during the course of a game. In order to file a protest, the procedure, as set forth in the NBA constitution, is as follows: "In order to protest against or appeal from the result of a game, notice thereof must be given to the Commissioner within forty-eight (48) hours after the conclusion of said game, by E-mail or fax, stating therein the grounds for such protest. No protest may be filed in connection with any game played during the regular season after midnight of the day of the last game of the regular schedule. A protest in connection with a playoff game must be filed not later than midnight of the day of the game protested. A game may be protested only by a Governor, Alternate Governor or Head Coach. The right of protest shall inure not only to the immediately allegedly aggrieved contestants, but to any other member who can show an interest in the grounds of protest and the results that might be attained if the protest were allowed. Each E-mail or fax of protest shall be immediately confirmed by letter and no protest shall be valid unless the letter of confirmation is accompanied by a check in the sum of $10,000 payable to the Association. If the member filing the protest prevails, the $10,000 is to be refunded. If the member does not prevail, the $10,000 is to be forfeited and retained in the Association treasury.

"Upon receipt of a protest, the Commissioner shall at once notify the member operating the opposing team in the game protested and require both of said members within five (5) days to file with him such evidence as he may desire bearing upon the issue. The Commissioner shall decide the question raised within five (5) days after receipt of such evidence."

## G. SHATTERING BACKBOARDS

Any player whose contact with the basket ring or backboard causes the backboard to shatter or makes the ring unplayable will be penalized in the following manner:

    (1) Pre-game and/or Half-time warm-ups—No penalty to be assessed by officials.

    (2) During the game—Non-unsportsmanlike conduct technical foul. Under NO circumstances will that player be ejected from the game.

The Commissioner will review all actions and plays involved in the shattering of a backboard.

## H. PLAYER/TEAM CONDUCT AND DRESS

(1) Each player when introduced, prior to the game, must be uniformly dressed.

(2) Players, coaches and trainers are to stand and line up in a dignified posture along the sidelines or on the foul line during the playing of the National Anthem.

(3) Coaches and assistant coaches must wear a sport coat or suit coat.

(4) While playing, players must keep their uniform shirts tucked into their pants, and no T-shirts are allowed.

(5) The only article bearing a commercial 'logo' which can be worn by players is their shoes.

## I. OFFENSIVE 3-SECONDS

The offensive player cannot be allowed in the 3-second lane for more than the allotted time. This causes the defensive player to 'hand-check' because he cannot control the offensive player for that extended period of time.

If the offensive player is in the 3-second lane for less than three seconds and receives the ball, he must make a move toward the hoop for the official to discontinue his three second count. If he attempts to back the defensive player down, attempting to secure a better position in relation to the basket, offensive three seconds or an offensive foul must be called. If he passes off and immediately makes a move out of the lane, there should be no whistle.

## J. PLAYER CONDUCT—SPECTATORS

Any coach, player or trainer who deliberately enters the spectator stands during the game will be automatically ejected and the incident reported by E-mail to the Commissioner. Entering the stands to keep a ball in play by a player or the momentum which carries the player into the stands is not considered deliberate. The first row of seats is considered the beginning of the stands.

## K. PUNCHING, FIGHTING AND ELBOW FOULS

Violent acts of any nature on the court will not be tolerated. Players involved in altercations will be ejected, fined and/or suspended.

Officials have been instructed to eject a player who throws a punch, whether or not it connects, or an elbow which makes contact above shoulder level. If elbow contact is shoulder level or below, it shall be left to the discretion of the official as to whether the player is ejected. Even if a punch or an elbow goes undetected by the officials during the game, but is detected during a review of a videotape, that player will be penalized.

There is absolutely no justification for fighting in an NBA game. The fact that you may feel provoked by another player is not an acceptable excuse. If a player takes it upon himself to retaliate, he can expect to be subject to appropriate penalties.

## L. EXPIRATION OF TIME

NO LESS THAN :00.3 must expire on the game clock when a ball is thrown inbounds and then hit instantly out-of-bounds. If less than :00.3 expires in such a situation, the timer will be instructed to deduct AT LEAST :00.3 from the game clock. If, in the judgment of the official, the play took longer than :00.3, he will instruct the timer to deduct more time. If less than :00.3 remain on the game clock when this situation occurs, the period is over.

NO LESS THAN :00.3 must expire on the game clock when a player secures possession of an inbounds pass and then attempts a field goal. If less than :00.3 expires in such a situation, the timer will be instructed to deduct AT LEAST :00.3 from the game clock. If less than :00.3 remain on the game clock when this situation occurs, the period is over, the field goal attempt will be disallowed immediately and instant replay will not be utilized.

This guideline shall apply to any field goal attempted by a player after he receives an inbounds pass, OTHER THAN what will be called, for this purpose, a "tip-in" or "alley oop."

A "tip-in" is defined as any action in which the ball is deflected, not controlled, by a player and then enters the basket ring. This type of action shall be deemed legal if :00.1 or more remains in a period.

A "high lob" is defined as a pass which is tipped by an offensive player while in mid-air, and is followed instantaneously by a field goal attempt. If the reception of the pass and the subsequent "slam dunk" is immediately adjacent to the basket ring, this type of action shall be deemed legal if :00.1 or more remains in a period. However, if the "high lob" attempt is a distance from the basket ring whereby the ball must be controlled in mid-air, either one-handed or two-handed, a minimum of :00.3 is necessary for a field goal to score if successful.

NO LESS than :00.3 must expire on the game clock when a player secures possession of an unsuccessful free throw attempt and immediately requests a timeout. If LESS than :00.3 expires in such a circumstance, the time on the game clock shall be reduced by at least :00.3. Therefore, if :00.3 OR LESS remain on the game clock when the above situation exists, and a player requests a timeout upon securing possession of the ball, the period is over.

During ANY regular or 20-second timeout taken during the FINAL minute of ANY period, the crew chief must meet with his fellow officials to discuss possible timing scenarios, fouls being taken if either team is under the penalty limit, number of timeouts, assistance by all officials on 3-point field goal attempts, rotation or away-from-the play foul.

Regardless of when the horn or red light operates to signify the end of period, the officials (as aided by instant replay, if required) will ultimately make the final decision whether to allow or disallow a successful field goal. THE CREW CHIEF MUST TAKE CHARGE OF THE SITUATION.

## M. VERBAL FAN INTERFERENCE

Any spectator who verbally abuses players and/or coaches in a manner which, in the opinion of the game officials, interferes with the ability of a coach to communicate with his players during the game and/or huddles, will, at the direction of the crew chief, be given one warning by a building security officer. If the same spectator continues to behave in a like manner, the crew chief shall direct a building security officer to eject the spectator from the arena.

## N. GUIDELINES FOR INFECTION CONTROL

If a player suffers a laceration or a wound where bleeding occurs, the officials shall suspend the game at the earliest appropriate time and allow a maximum of 30 seconds for treatment. After that time, the head coach shall be informed that he has the option to substitute for the player, call a regular timeout or a 20-second timeout. If a substitute replaces the player, the opposing team shall be allowed to substitute one player. The injured player may return to the game when he has received appropriate treatment by medical staff personnel.

If the player returns to the game, the officials shall make certain that any lesion, wound or dermatitis is covered with a dressing that will prevent contamination to and/or from other sources. A wrist or sweat band is not considered a suitable bandage.

If the injured player is awarded a free throw attempt(s) as a result of a personal foul, or is involved in a jump ball, the injured player will be given 30 seconds for treatment. If the treatment is not completed, play will resume and will then be suspended at the first appropriate time.

Mandatory timeouts shall not be granted during a suspension of play unless the offensive team calls a 20-second timeout. If the suspension of play is for a defensive player, a mandatory timeout shall not be granted if the defensive team calls a 20-second timeout. In that case, only the bleeding player may be replaced and, if so, the opposing team is permitted one substitute.

If treatment is not completed within the allotted time, the head coach may call another timeout or substitute for the injured player. Substitutes are permitted consistent with existing rules on substitution.

If a team has no timeouts remaining when play is suspended, the officials will allow 30 seconds for appropriate treatment. If the treatment is not completed in accordance with paragraph two above, the injured player must be removed immediately. ONLY the injured player on that team may be removed from the game under these circumstances. If so, the opponent may also substitute one player.

The offensive team will receive a full eight seconds to advance the ball into the frontcourt. The 24 second clock will remain as is or reset to 14, whichever is greater.

## O. DEAD BALL, LIVE BALL, BALL IS ALIVE

After the ball has been dead, it is put into play by a jump ball, throw-in or a free throw attempt. The game clock does not start until the ball is legally touched on the court by a player. However, any floor violation or personal foul which may occur will be penalized.

The ball is live when it is placed at the disposal of the thrower-in, free throw shooter or is tossed by the official on a jump ball. Illegal contact, which occurs prior to the ball becoming live, will be ignored if it is not unsportsmanlike.

The ball is alive when it is legally tapped by one of the participants of a jump ball, released by a thrower-in or released on a free throw attempt that will remain in play.

## P. TAUNTING

If a player blatantly taunts an opponent, a technical foul shall be assessed. The opponent WILL NOT, automatically, be assessed a technical foul. His behavior will be the determining factor.

Simultaneous taunting is a verbal altercation. Verbal altercations and unsportsmanlike conduct will be administered as a double technical foul and no free throws will be attempted.

Technical fouls assessed to opposing teams during the same dead ball and prior to the administering of any free throw attempt for the first technical foul, shall be interpreted as a double technical foul.

A PLAYER(S) GUILTY OF TAUNTING MUST BE SINGLED OUT AND PENALIZED.

If a previous unsportsmanlike act has been committed and if this situation is BLATANT, a technical foul must be assessed and the guilty player(s) must be ejected.

| GOALTENDING | ILLEGAL DRIBBLE | DIRECTION OF PLAY |
|---|---|---|
|  |  |  |
| "Flag" from wrist | Patting motion call team color | Point · Direction call team color |

| TIME-IN | TIME-OUT | PERSONAL FOUL |
|---|---|---|
|  |  |  |
| Chop hand to side | Open palm | Clenched fist |

| HOLDING | LOOSE BALL FOUL | ILLEGAL USE OF HANDS |
|---|---|---|
|  |  |  |
| Signal foul: grasp wrist | Extended arms to shoulder level | Signal foul: strike wrist |

## TO DESIGNATE OFFENDER

Hold up number of player

## HAND CHECKING

Arm straight out opposite arm grabbing wrist

## ILLEGAL FOREARM

Arm bent 90° in front of body

## CHARGING

Clenched fist

## DOUBLE FOUL

Cross clenched fists above head

## ILLEGAL SCREEN OUT-OF-BOUNDS

Arms outstretched and crossed in front of chest

## 20-SECOND TIME-OUT

Hands touching shoulders

## PUSHING

Signal foul: imitate push

## BLOCKING

Hands on hips

## TECHNICAL FOUL

Form T

## CANCEL SCORE CANCEL PLAY

Shift arms across body

## 3-SECOND OFFENSIVE VIOLATION

Fingers sidewards

## 4-SECOND VIOLATION

Tap head
signal '24'

## FOR 3-PT. FIELD GOAL

Official will raise
one arm on attempt

If goal is successful
raise the other arm

BASKET INTERFERENCE

Rotate finger
wipe out basket

TRAVELING

Rotate fists

JUMP BALL

Thumbs up

DEFENSIVE 3-SECOND
VIOLATION

Chop down two times
followed by technical foul signal